LEGACY
ON ICE

LEGACY ON ICE

*Blake Geoffrion and the
Fastest Game on Earth*

SAM JEFFERIES

Foreword by John Buccigross

THE UNIVERSITY OF WISCONSIN PRESS

The University of Wisconsin Press
728 State Street, Suite 443
Madison, Wisconsin 53706
uwpress.wisc.edu

Gray's Inn House, 127 Clerkenwell Road
London ECIR 5DB, United Kingdom
eurospanbookstore.com

Printed in the United States of America
This book may be available in a digital edition.

Library of Congress Cataloging-in-Publication Data
Names: Jefferies, Sam, author.
Title: Legacy on ice : Blake Geoffrion and the fastest game on earth / Sam Jefferies.
Description: Madison, Wisconsin : The University of Wisconsin Press, 2023.
Identifiers: LCCN 2023015008 | ISBN 9780299344900 (hardcover)
Subjects: LCSH: Geoffrion, Blake. | Hockey players—United States—Biography.
Classification: LCC GV848.5.G46 J44 2023 | DDC 796.962092
[B]—dc23/eng/20230425
LC record available at https://lccn.loc.gov/2023015008

To
LEAH *and* WILLIAM

CONTENTS

PREFACE

The story of Blake Geoffrion is both extraordinary and prosaic. It's a fascinating personal tale: the scion of a family at the center of the French-Canadian hockey nobility grows up in relative anonymity in the US South, then rises once again to prominence atop the world of North American men's hockey, only to have his rise cut short by horrifying injury.

It does not end with him lifting the Stanley Cup or standing awash in Olympic glory. It is, however, a story of remarkable coincidence that, when overlaid on the major events of the hockey world over the past three decades, offers a glimpse into not just when but why.

This book is a product of dozens of interviews with coaches, players, mothers, fathers, and brothers; trainers and equipment managers; executives and scouts; beat writers and broadcasters; fans, friends, hockey historians, union organizers, and bartenders. It relies on firsthand accounts, in-game footage and on-camera interviews, historical analysis and contemporary news coverage. The sourcing is necessarily diverse because the story is not simple.

Blake repeatedly found himself at the convergence of events, at some times leading, at others unwittingly participating. As a teenager, he landed in the center of USA Hockey's struggle to regain its Lake Placid luster after the 1980 Miracle on Ice. As a college player, he became a four-year superstar at a dynastic program at the tail end of a half-century era of four-year superstars and dynastic programs. As the first homegrown NHL player in the South and also the fourth generation of his family to wear an NHL sweater, he was simultaneously the newest of the new and the oldest of the old. And as he rose through the ranks of the game, the undercurrent of professional hockey's labor negotiations dragged him along with it.

His journey brought him back to the cradle of North American hockey, but it began in the most improbable of places: Williamson County, Tennessee.

ACKNOWLEDGMENTS

The writing of this book would not have been possible without the generous help of the Geoffrion family, and I am forever grateful to Blake, Katelyn, Danny, and Kelly for sharing their most treasured memories with me. Nor would it have come to life without the support of my own parents, who read to me endlessly and then left me alone to find my own literary way, which led me to the book you are holding now.

Thank you to Mike Eaves and Jeff Jackson and Bob Mancini and Ron DeGregorio and Rob Andringa and all the coaches, players, trainers, reporters, announcers, fans, and many others who spent time with me during the research process, and to my aunt and uncle Jane and Jim Jefferies, who listened to every update and never shied away from one more conversation about Badger hockey.

For encouragement and support, thank you to Beau Tremitiere, who told me, "Enough with the articles, it's time for a book," and to Brendan O'Meara, who rescued a first draft with a barrel's worth of red ink.

And finally, and most importantly, to my wife, who has lived with a sleep-deprived writer and a too-soon-retired hockey player for four long years. Thank you.

FOREWORD

John Buccigross, ESPN

From the moment our children first slide into this world, we as parents do all that we can to make the ride even smoother. We round out corners. We sandpaper, flatten, and refine. We strive to appease the dangerous edges, control the uncontrollable, and make every fall soft and pillowy as our children flit about in this unpredictable and coarse world.

Some of us will sign our kids up for difficult and somewhat dangerous sport like hockey to counter life's overprotected playpens and to teach our kids that actual life is actually hard. We parents know that real adult life, like hockey, is lived in the corners, on the edge, and there are few soft falls.

Hockey is hard.

Blake Geoffrion is well aware of the inherent dangers of the game. They're in his bloodlines, the bruised and battered elephant in the room.

Hockey is the fastest, toughest, most difficult game. A dangerous, perilous pursuit sliding along that fine line between classical music ballet and punk rock anarchy—from the orchestra pit to the mosh pit in the blink of a bloody eye.

Geoffrion's great-grandfather, the legendary and dominant Howie Morenz, was one of the most electrifying players of the 1920s and early '30s. In a game in what was to be his final NHL season in 1937, Morenz broke his leg in four places. While recuperating in St. Luke Hospital,

Morenz died a little more than a month after his injury, his life shock-ingly ended by an undetected blood clot. He was thirty-four.

Blake's grandfather, Bernie "Boom Boom" Geoffrion, broke his nose nine times and received four hundred stitches in his sixteen-season Hall of Fame career. Once, during a Canadiens practice in 1958, Boom Boom collided with a teammate and collapsed a few seconds later, his intestine perforated. He was rushed to the hospital for emergency surgery and given last rites at twenty-seven. He survived, returning to the ice five weeks later to help lead Montreal to another Stanley Cup victory.

While Blake's father, Danny Geoffrion, escaped a major on-ice injury during his playing career, Blake would not escape the dangers of the game. With the NHL lockout canceling the first month of the 2012–13 regular season and with no end in sight, 18,582 hockey-starved fans filled the Canadiens home arena, the Bell Centre, on Friday, November 9, 2012, to watch Montreal's minor league team, the Hamilton Bulldogs of the American Hockey League (AHL), host the Syracuse Crunch. Blake was a member of the Bulldogs following a trade to the organization that retired his grandfather's and great-grandfather's numbers.

During this AHL game, Blake Geoffrion was skating with the puck at full speed up the left wing side a couple of feet from the boards. At about the red line, he peeked over to see who was coming. It was six-foot-two, 215-pound defenseman Jean-Philippe Côté, who hit Geoffrion with such force that his body twirled counterclockwise like a windmill, his right skate at least seven feet in the air at its peak, his head like the hand on a clock going from twelve (when hit) to three (his torso parallel to the ice) to six (his head smacking the ice about a foot from the boards).

But before Geoffrion's head hit the ice, Côté's razor-sharp skate blade carved into the bone two inches above Geoffrion's left ear. Although he didn't know it at the time, Blake's hockey career was over in that instant.

Sam Jefferies has chosen an apt subject for his hockey story. Despite its disappointing ending, Blake Geoffrion has lived a life rich with fam-ily and love. His unique hockey lineage and on-ice success while grow-ing up in of all places, Nashville, Tennessee, is a worthy story to tell.

What I find even more interesting is Blake's spirit and personality, which mirror this game of hockey we love. He has an infectious zest for life, filled with enthusiasm and ideas. His perceptions and judgments make him an excellent hang to converse on a variety of subjects. He could be a president or general manager of a hockey team on the business side or the hockey operations side—maybe at the same time. His energy and how he connects seem to present him with limitless options for succeeding in life.

His hockey story from the past is rich and worthy of the detail in these pages. His hockey future? A mystery for now. But, after reading this book, I think you might agree that Blake has got more to give and that a new, unknown hockey chapter remains to be written. And anything is possible.

LEGACY ON ICE

PROLOGUE

One Night in Montreal

This is hockey in pure form, hockey for its own sake, stripped of the bells and whistles of international attention and the always-looming specter of a $64.3 million salary cap. It is November 9, 2012, and by all rights twenty-one thousand rabid supporters of the Montreal Canadiens should be pouring into the Bell Centre for an early season matchup. That's what Habs fans do in November, right? Don an authentic team sweater, comforting in its weight, bright white letters on the back set against a rich shade of red fabric, paired with omnipresent fur-lined Sorel boots and a knitted toque adorned with the classic Canadiens *C* to top off the whole beautiful outfit. Down one last glass of Molson's at McLean's Pub before spilling out onto Peel Street to join the throngs marching toward that cathedral of hockey with *Centre Bell* spelled out in towering blue letters above the entrance. Bronzed Canadiens legends, eternally frozen in poses of glory, watch over the masses shuffling shoulder to shoulder, dressed identically, pushing impatiently through the turnstiles.

But tonight, no National Hockey League superstars will take to the ice. No television boom mikes will catch the sound of skates scraping or sticks slapping, and the luxury suites will be empty of their usual suit-and-tie-clad business executives. A different kind of spectacle awaits the fans of Montreal, La Belle Ville. Tonight, the Hamilton Bulldogs, Montreal's minor league affiliate, will face off against the Syracuse Crunch in a rare farm-team clash on the big stage. Minor league squads seldom get this kind of ice time in hockey's biggest markets—maybe once a year if they're lucky. Young prospects and aging journeymen colliding in a display of the unvarnished, genuine, love-the-game-or-leave-your-seat competition that has enraptured Canadians since the days before television and instant replay. Tonight's ticket promises only one thing, but it's what the Quebecois have been starved of for two long, terrible months: hockey.

The NHL lockout is fifty-four days old, and every fan in the arena is grumbling about the grim prospects for a resolution. It's the second lockout in eight years, and millions of US and Canadian fans have watched their beloved players flee overseas to play in Russia, Sweden, and the Czech Republic, where leagues have embraced them with open arms. They've seen their kids lose ice time to professionals, who rent full rinks to stay limber while they wait out the dispute. But this evening's game offers a brief salvation, an escape from endless talk-radio bashing, and a chance to see prospects up close. In the lineup for Hamilton is Brendan Gallagher, the five-foot-nine ball of energy who dazzled as a winger for Team Canada at the World Juniors last spring. Prized prospect Nathan Beaulieu anchors the Bulldogs' blue line. And center Blake Geoffrion will be hunched over the face-off circle, the six-foot-one bruiser whose last name still makes the ears of every old-timer perk up, evoking the golden age of Le Club de Hockey Canadien.

Blake's presence in the lineup means more than just another strong, fast, two-way forward to anchor the Bulldogs' offensive attack. For the fourth time in the past century, a member of the Geoffrion-Morenz hockey dynasty will lace up his skates in Montreal. Montreal, the town where Blake's father was a first-round draft pick, where his grandfather, Boom Boom, invented the slap shot, and where his great-grandfather, Howie, earned a spot in the Hall of Fame as hockey's original superstar. The eyes of the hockey world have followed Blake, unblinkingly, since long before his first NHL game. This night is no exception, even if it's only a forgettable matchup between farm system players eating minutes until they get a shot at the Big Show. Stitched on the back of Blake's white Bulldogs sweater is the number 57—5 for Boom Boom, 7 for

Howie. For Blake and for the restless fans craning their necks toward the blur of bodies and sticks and one elusive puck, every shift is significant.

There are no throwaway games in the pursuit of a legacy.

∽

It can't be just another game in the schedule, not with that crowd, in that city, not after so many weeks of waiting and watching and wondering. Not for Blake Geoffrion or any other player on the bus up from Hamilton, Ontario, where the Bulldogs suffered a 3–0 loss to the same Crunch team at the Dog Pound, their usual home arena, only two days before. It's about a six-hour drive from Hamilton to Montreal, where the franchise management and the media—the whole hockey world, really—awaits their arrival. Friday night, on the big stage. A chance to shine! This lockout will end someday, and when it does, the suits who shuffle players between franchises will recall nights like tonight. And every man on the team knows it; a restlessness seeps through the bus, fogging the windows with every audible exhale. The players incessantly fiddle with their phones as tires eat up the asphalt beneath them—listening to music, scrolling Twitter, or checking Yahoo's Puck Daddy blog, where hockey's blogger in chief Greg Wyshynski has created "The Vent" to host livid rants from fans of all ages. ESPN.com's headline article, "NHL, Union Resume Talks," offers little insight on the standoff between the owners and the players' union, hosting instead another solemn recitation of canned statements and speculation. Other media outlets have taken a different angle to keep fans engaged. Pat Hickey of the *Montreal Gazette* has been covering a fictional Canadiens season, complete with simulated games and manufactured quotes, and even skeptical readers have to be impressed by Andrei Markov's dramatically improved English.

Hickey's "coverage" might offer amusing distractions for Quebec's ravenous hockey fans, but it does nothing for the dozens of men whose livelihoods are caught in limbo or for their families. For every Bulldog yearning for a call-up and for the players still governed by entry-level contracts with a maximum salary of $70,000 per year, no distraction will suffice.

Blake sits in the middle of the bus, headphones on. One long leg sprawls out into the carpeted aisle. His parents are coming to the game tonight, in the town where his father was born, learned to skate, and was drafted into the Canadiens organization, and then they're off to Boston, where Blake's two brothers will play together in a collegiate tournament the next evening. For Danny and Kelly Geoffrion, tonight is another game among thousands, special but sometimes hard to distinguish after years spent in chilled arenas across the globe. They've always been rink-side, cheering and cajoling Blake as he climbed the ladder of hockeydom from his childhood in Tennessee onward. First it was youth hockey, watching Mini-Mites careening around the rinks of suburban Nashville. Then on to the frozen bleachers of summer camps and prep school and eventually the US National Team Development Program, where the gangly teenager served up one goal after another en route to a gold medal for Team USA at the 2006 U18 World Championships. Then Madison, Wisconsin, and four years of elite Division I play for the University of Wisconsin Badgers, including a magical senior season that ended with a trip to the national championship and the Hobey Baker Award, the Heisman Trophy of college hockey. Blake was the first Badger honored as the nation's best college hockey player. And his folks were there to see it. Award ceremonies and adulation and national media attention followed, a blur, interviews and questions and comparisons to his family lineage, a whirlwind of distractions until finally pro hockey, that elusive dream that had consumed two decades of locker-room chatter and scheming around the kitchen table.

Blake had already played in the league for parts of two seasons with the Nashville Predators, a franchise located eleven miles from his hometown of Brentwood, Tennessee. When he was suiting up in a Preds jersey, it was nearly guaranteed that at least one parent would be there to watch. But the previous February, as Montreal eyed an abysmal finish in the basement of the Northeast division, the team moved veteran defenseman Hal Gill to the surging Predators in exchange for minor league forward Robert Slaney, a second-round pick, and the opportunity to return Blake Geoffrion to his ancestral hockey home.

Blake had been surprised at the time—he'd skated his socks off for Nashville and loved being the team's first homegrown player—but heading north, to play in the beating heart of hockey-mad Canada, was nearly as good. Every game sold out, the biggest arena in the NHL, tickets as scarce as palm trees in Nova Scotia. Even the country's prime minister has written a book on the sport. Everyone has a blog, a podcast, an opinion on who plays on what line when, whether Bobby Hull or Maurice "Rocket" Richard was the better player, and whether a Canadian team will ever again win a Stanley Cup. Endless speculation on the Geoffrion legacy percolates in the crisp air. Can Blake shoot like his Pappy? Skate like his great-grandfather? Become a professional-level version of the hitting, checking, cleanup-goal-scoring stalwart everyone has heard so much about since he exchanged his Badger uniform for a pro sweater? The final months of last season were a tease, one lovely Geoffrion-scored goal in a March 10 game against Vancouver before the ugly season ended mercifully three weeks later. He'd offered fans a glimpse of his potential. They knew—and he knew—that he'd only scratched the surface.

Then came the lockout and the weekly spectacle of dueling press conferences staged by intractable negotiators. Frustration and uncertainty chiseled away at the optimism he'd taken for granted. His path to professional hockey had always moved upward, one step after another. This was a new feeling. It wasn't pleasant.

"Is it time for us to give up hope? Is it time for us to acknowledge that maybe Lassie isn't just sleeping, she's dead?" queried the *Gazette*'s James Mennie mournfully on the paper's podcast, echoing the defeatism that had permeated hockey's millions of fans and players. "If there's a light at the end of the tunnel, it's probably a locomotive."

October has passed with barely any contact between the two sides, and November isn't looking much better. The roots of the lockout lie deep in the earth. Two years earlier, the NHL Players' Association had hired as its executive director former Major League Baseball union chief Donald Fehr, the "dour face of players not playing,"[1] who had earned a steely reputation as a hard-line negotiator over nearly three decades of labor disputes. Fehr's impervious disregard for media criticism was legendary: he was there to do the job, not make friends. He stood firm as the 1994 World Series was canceled, and the strike eventually ended in a resounding success for the players' union. The National Labor Relations Board found the owners' salary cap illegal, scabs were tossed out of spring training, and nine more years would pass before the league implemented a new luxury tax on overspending teams. In just a few months, Fehr had become an internationally recognized superstar of the labor movement.

The players' association was notoriously disorganized, and Fehr, no more than a casual hockey fan, was brought aboard in 2009 to clean up the shop, twenty-five months before the current collective-bargaining agreement was set to expire at 11:59 p.m. on September 15, 2012. For anyone unaccustomed to the puttering world of labor negotiations, two-plus years seemed an eternity. But for Fehr and the hundreds of players he represented, the clock was ticking.

The summer of 2012 had dragged along with little reason for optimism and no real progress. In late July, as the ridiculous mounted, the NHL had sent the players' association seventy-six thousand pages of financial documents to justify its initial offer and "help" the union prepare its counter. Sniping in the press quickly became all-out warfare. On Friday, August 17, Fehr growled snark into a conference-call microphone, "Do we have an equal say on anything? That's what a partnership normally implies." Although the league offered a new proposal less than two weeks later, the lockout drumbeat was quickly building into a crescendo.

At the core of the dispute were two issues: the players' share of so-called hockey-related-revenue and players' salaries, which must fit under a salary cap of $64.3 million per year that owners claimed provided certainty against inflated salaries. League owners, represented by much-loathed NHL commissioner Gary Bettman, wanted a greater share of that revenue; the players didn't want to give it up. And if a lockout occurred, the minor leagues would continue to play, absorbing the young NHL stars still governed by the fine print in their entry-level contracts, which allowed the players to skate for American Hockey League (AHL) teams.

AHL players in 2012 were much better off than their minor league baseball counterparts during the 1994 Fehr-led strike. After that season was abruptly canceled in mid-August, some owners fielded teams of replacement players, mostly career minor leaguers strung along by the promise of meager salaries even as they were ostracized by the ballplayers who wouldn't cross picket lines. Thanks to the Professional Hockey Players' Association, the only minor league union in North America, AHL players were guaranteed a minimum salary of $42,375 a season, decent housing, and per diem payments that made the barnstorming lifestyle livable. First organized in the 1960s by Doug Messier, father of Hall of Famer Mark Messier, the Professional Hockey Players' Association originally sought to guarantee that minor league players had decent health insurance—not for broken bones or missing teeth, although those demanded their share of medical attention, but because the players' wives were leaving their husbands midseason to return to Canada to deliver their babies, and something had to change. It was a good deal for the journeymen, the longtime minor league players who endured season after season, occasionally plugging a hole in the NHL lineup but generally relegated to hockey's second tier by virtue of age or ability.

But for the future stars, still blessed with youth and speed and optimism and most of their teeth, still driven by the phantom hum of an engraving pen gouging fresh names into Lord Stanley's Cup, an extended stay in the AHL was a tripping hazard at best.

Khhissssss. The brakes release, and the Bulldogs' garish red bus shudders downward, sinking toward the frigid concrete in jerky motions, groaning under the weight of twenty players and their skates, sticks, helmets, shoulder pads, elbow pads, shin pads, goalie pads, breezers, mouth guards, towels, socks, practice pucks, sweaters, trainers, and coaches. Another *khhissss* and the doors pop open, one player after another swinging out onto the curb, snorting plumes of steam into the afternoon air. The windows are fogged, streaked with rivulets, tallies on a cellblock wall for Geoffrion, Gallagher, and the other prospects trapped in this minor league purgatory as the lockout reaches its fifty-fourth day. Before them, the Bell Centre stands in concrete enormity. Taunting them. It should be a representation of the NHL and their ascendancy to the highest level of competition the sport has to offer. Tonight, it's a reminder of the uncertainty ruling their professional careers.

Each player shoulders an enormous black equipment bag as he strides toward the concrete behemoth casting shadows over L'Avenue des Canadiens-de-Montréal. A few step awkwardly—duckfooted off the ice, stumbling occasionally as if they had toe-picked late in the third period—as they walk across latticed red bricks and cement toward the players' entrance, passing one giant red, white, and blue C and another and another. This is the home of the Canadiens. *Les* Canadiens. The team of Stanley Cup supremacy stretching all the way back to 1916 and the Great War. The team of those magical two decades when its unstoppable force crushed opponents; the team of Maurice Richard's goal-scoring brilliance and Doug Harvey's defensive stinginess and then of Boom Boom's slap shot and Ken Dryden's unwavering dependability between the pipes—champions in '65, '66, '68, '69, '71, '73, '76, '77, '78, '79. Of Patrick Roy and two overtime wins in '93 and delirious mobs screaming his name throughout the streets of Montreal. The games, the goals, the madness of the fans. Even on a night like this, without the Canadiens' public relations department bludgeoning heartsick fans with another wrenching tribute video on the Jumbotron, emotion and fanaticism ooze from the walls.

Eager to set aside league politics and the memory of Wednesday's loss to the Crunch, Blake can't help but embrace the romanticism of the moment. Sitting in the Canadiens' locker room, team logos dotting the wall above his head, he settles into his pregame routine. Once, twice, three times, four times he wraps fresh tape along the length of his stick blade, the perfect balance of cushion to settle skittering passes and rigidity to fire pucks across the ice, down the boards, past the defenders, into the soft, white netting beckoning from behind the goaltender. Cotton squeezes tight against his fingers as he laces up, leaning from the wooden bench, head down, focused on the ritual of preparation. It is a process with its own rhythm and flow, a mind-clearing exercise more calming than Sunday prayer. Locker room chatter drones around him, but Blake hears none of it.

His old man would be watching tonight, always supportive, never satisfied. So, in spirit, would his grandfather and his great-grandfather, whose retired numbers hang from the rafters of the storied arena. A leering cartoon Bulldog, bedecked with a spiked collar and half-crunched bone, is stamped on his chest. The Hamilton logo is only a distraction. The Montreal *C* on each shoulder is what matters, famous emblems borrowed from the parent club for which he should, in a fair world, be suiting up tonight. But the world isn't fair. Blake thrusts his head into his white helmet, its straps hanging loosely, flapping against his jaws, and joins the line of teammates marching upward toward the blaring music, the screaming fans, the waiting ice.

~

Mesdames et messieurs, ladies and gentlemen de Montréal, sus Bull-dooooogs de Hamilton!

In the booth tonight sits Derek Wills of Hamilton's Funny 820 Radio. The broadcast simulcasts on Montreal's TSN 920. No color commentary, just a one-man minor league show for the folks back home.

. . . and in goal for your Bulldogs, No. 29, RRRRRRobert Mayer!

The announcer shouts over the hammering of 1980s rock, a sea of toques bobbing and booted feet pounding against the concrete terracing, fifteen thousand typically mild-mannered Canadians scream and whoop, desperate to slake their thirst for hockey. Everyone stands, peering down at the backs of the men racing in a circle in front of the net. The Habs fans can easily pick out last year's rising stars—Aaron Palushaj, Frédéric St-Denis, and Michael Blunden, already well known to the Bell Centre regulars. And Blake Geoffrion, *there he is!* The big center whizzes around the ice and rips pucks at the net—wrist shots, slap shots, backhand, forehand—his torso draped in Bulldog white, the blue numbers sprawled across his broad back. A Geoffrion back in Montreal, where he belongs; Boom Boom's grandson, home again. The music pounds, strobe lights flicker in the darkened arena, reflected in the glow of the Jumbotron, shimmering on the ice already gouged with every dig of every skate; hands clap and voices bellow, drowning out the slap of graphite on puck after puck.

The place hums with energy, pulses in anticipation. *Can you feel it?* Someone finally kills the music, and the boys line up on their respective blue lines, shuffling anxiously through the national anthem, the gaze of thousands fixated on five strapping skaters and a maskless goalie even as the singer saunters out onto a square of black carpet placed in front of the Bulldogs' bench for this occasion. And then the place erupts again! *O Canada! Terre de nos aïeux, ton front est ceint de fleurons glorieux . . .* Fans roar, belting it out, and they don't miss a beat when the singer switches to English in that Montreal tradition. *God keep our land, glorious and free, O Canada! we stand on guard for thee!*

On display are a people proudly proclaiming their love for the sport and for the North, the frozen prairies and ponds and lakes and rivers that had first given the world the game, this game, *the greatest game.* And after the ceremonial puck drop and the local dignitaries wave to a politely applauding crowd, it's time for the real thing. No more throbbing music or gimmicky entreaties to a restless crowd. Two players at center ice, hands low, sticks down, heads nearly touching.

The referee drops the puck.

Blake's stick handle raps against the white polyethylene of the boards; he leans forward on the red bench, chewing his mouthguard, watching, listening to the *fffwwsshhh!* of skaters streaking by. It's eleven minutes into the first period, and he hadn't felt too good during his first two shifts. Maybe it was the watchful eyes of his father and the Habs' executives or the lingering hangover from Wednesday's loss, but he hasn't put it together quite yet this evening, and neither have his teammates. Sloppy hockey so far, no clear control, a turnover, an errant pass, another turnover, fans groaning as each squandered chance mocks their collective desire for a smooth rush down the ice. But then the call—*Change 'em up!*—and Blake is over the side of the boards again, and this time it feels smooth. He powers through his strides, muscling out a few Syracuse players in the Bulldogs' half of the rink. Hamilton winger Mike Blunden hits Blake with a clean pass, *whriss* from left to right across the defensive zone, and he thumps the blade of his stick as he starts to move forward, straight out of a practice drill.

And then he's off! Blake races along the boards, long arms and legs flying as skate blades dig into the ice. Whipping himself along, his left arm brushes the glass as fans leave their seats and watch No. 57, with only one hand on the stick, carry the puck forward comfortably, powerfully, one, two, three strides propel him along the boards, head down, open ice in sight as teammates and opponents swarm behind him, trying to catch him, no one noticing the blue body of Jean-Philippe Côté zipping backward across the ice toward him . . .

Big collision, a hip check from Côté on the near boards, Blake goes down . . .

Not the thud of bodies crunching that hockey fans savor, but a sick *chwitt*, like a steel blade slicing into an overfilled tire. Blake's body careens clockwise through the air, limbs flailing, before crumpling to the ice, motionless. Blunden comes ripping across, smashing Côté against the boards; Blunden drops his stick and shoves the opposing player backward.

Blake still isn't moving, isn't rising to join the scuffle. His head rests still, forehead pressed against the ice. And the blood is pooling quickly.

Boos rain down from the crowd. Then, hidden behind the jersey pulling and jostling, Blake pulls himself onto his hands and knees. He pauses, gathering strength, oblivious to the scuffle feet from him. Finally he stands, hunched over, clutching his head, pausing again, his body shuddering slightly. Still bent double, he glides over to the Hamilton bench. His hair, matted and dripping, hangs limply before his face, and in a second he's off the ice, shuffling down the tunnel to the locker room. Two rink attendants in dark tracksuits skate toward the spot of the collision. They pause briefly, staring down at the stain, and then begin to use the gardening tools they've carried with them to scrape the ice clean of Blake's blood.

chapter 1

WILLIAMSON COUNTY

Williamson County, Tennessee, is about as far from hockey country as you can get. The ponds don't freeze in the winter, and the driveways aren't cluttered with nets and sticks and scuffed tennis balls in the summer. Few parents are seen hawking old gloves and skates at offseason garage sales in this enclave of suburban Nashville. In fact, garage sales are a bit gauche for the Brentwood-Franklin corridor, the beating heart of this staunchly conservative, low-tax/no-tax slice of the American landscape that's home to more guitar-shaped swimming pools than ice rinks. Even the politics are polite: the Williamson County Republican Women's Club cordially rotates its monthly luncheon between Lillie Belle's on Franklin's oh-so-cute Main Street ("an oasis of Southern hospitality!") and the Brentwood Country Club, tucked fittingly along Country Club Drive. Residents of Williamson County for nearly thirty years, the Geoffrions still seem to be blinking their French-Canadian eyelashes in shock in the dazzling southern sunshine.

The county has been well-to-do and aristocratic for longer than hockey has been played in North America. Fertile agricultural land and a relatively small group of landowners led to the rise of the area's great plantations, which dotted the countryside at comfortable distances and anchored the local economy for the first half of the nineteenth century. Nestled in mansions in the white-columned Greek Revival style, the plantation families spread gentility throughout the antebellum social scene. All this grand wealth was built on the unpaid labor of an enormous and largely silent community of African Americans. By 1860, enslaved persons outnumbered white residents of the county, and the ratio was even higher on the big plantations. For white citizens, top-dollar private schooling was available to the local elite, just as it is today, although public schooling eventually emerged in the region during Reconstruction. Even President Andrew Jackson, whose pugilistic populism and impoverished roots frightened the landed gentry of his home state, made occasional trips to the area, always spending the night at the famed Carnton Plantation outside of Franklin.

Emancipation came as a shock to Middle Tennessee, the wealthiest of the state's three grand divisions, and it upended the local plantation economy. But even the Thirteenth Amendment wouldn't prevent Williamson from eventually reassuming its place as one of the wealthiest counties in America. Now home to a golfer's paradise of private country clubs, manicured greens and weedless fairways encroach on the old encampment sites of the Army of Tennessee. Golf shares the spotlight with the more respectable sports of the prep school world—the elite Brentwood Academy alone claims dozens of state championships in track and field, baseball, and football, programs generously supported by the booster club's art show, held annually the first week of December. Being a player's parent is a status symbol across the South, especially in football-obsessed Tennessee, where locals say the year has only two seasons: football and spring practice. In the 1990s, when the squeaky-clean, Tennessee Orange–clad visage of Peyton Manning graced bedroom walls in Brentwood and Franklin, hockey was a bit too blue-collar to fit comfortably into genteel conversation in the "most conservative-friendly county in America."[1]

"Hockey has always been a stolen game, a suppressed game, on the edge of society's norms, dirty, lower class," wrote Stephen Marche in *The Meaning of Hockey*. His description of the sport is enough to make the polo-shirt-wearing legions of suburban Nashville shudder with distaste. Hockey has always been rough around the edges, the purview of kids who could escape unsupervised to frozen ponds while their parents labored through another shift. Gordie Howe, known as Mr. Hockey, famously scrounged his first pair of skates from a sack of used items that a cash-strapped neighbor had sold to Gordie's mother for fifty cents during the Great Depression. From those meager beginnings in rural Saskatchewan, Howe would go on to become an international phenomenon, a toothless poster child for the sport, recognized and beloved by fans around the world. His game was anchored in temerity, a style of play stamped into skaters from rural Canada, from Rust Belt America, and from the same soot-stained, industrial New England towns that also churned out prizefighters by the barrelful.

Long, cold days on the windswept ponds of the North forced these players to skate faster and hit harder to stay warm. Deft stickhandling and straight shooting were a must because any puck fired into the snowbanks wouldn't be found until spring thaw. And working-class parents loved the game just as deeply. For half a century, steel mill workers in Pennsylvania and longshoremen in Boston packed third-shift bars to trade views on the goalies and goons whose sport mirrored their gritty lives. "Blue-collar hockey" remains an oft-used term among broadcasters and sports page pundits; it refers to players who abandon finesse for a more rough and rugged style of play, grinding it out on the boards, making every puck count and every opponent pay. "Lunchpail wingers" are those who forgo polish for tough but effective play on both ends of the ice. Even as fistfights have fallen out of fashion as a socially acceptable way to settle a dispute, the punishment for dropping the gloves onto the ice and punching an opposing player in the face is still only five minutes off the ice. In a sport that centers on a rubber puck being flung at speeds over ninety miles per hour, face masks remain optional at the professional level. It is a dangerous and messy game, requiring a certain disdain for pretty smiles. Members of the working class in the United States and Canada have been screaming for more for a hundred years.

Down in Williamson and Maury Counties, which share the town of Spring Hill and its thirty-four thousand residents, many local hockey boosters are as blue-collar as the roots of their beloved sport. In 1990, eight years before the first puck was dropped at a Nashville Predators' game, General Motors opened a new $3.5 billion plant to assemble Saturn cars and sport utility vehicles on the site of the old Haynes Haven horse farm, up the road from the historic Rippavilla Plantation and its Greek Revival mansion. With the plant's ribbon cutting came six thousand new jobs. Because GM had a national collective-bargaining agreement with the United Auto Workers (UAW) union, those positions would be filled by the time-honored rules of seniority; long-serving union members from Michigan and Wisconsin would be offered the first jobs, and on down the line.

In antiunion Tennessee, where right-to-work legislation meant to break the back of organized labor passed in 1947 and where union membership is less than half the national rate, this repulsed the local aristocracy. Here was another affront to the local economic system, this time in the form of a distinctly northern style of workforce organization and profit sharing, in a part of the country where some still refer to the Civil War as the War of Northern Aggression. In Williamson County, where the average household income is $104,367 and the GOP's Ronald Reagan Dinner is a can't-miss event, the plant's arrival resembled yet another Yankee invasion.

The UAW has been a powerful political and cultural force in the Midwest since the early twentieth century, and Red Wings and Black-hawks stickers have been sharing bumper space with *Union Yes!* decals for nearly as long. Hockey and union membership seem inherently to run together, like playmakers and open ice or cold beer and barstool storytelling after three periods of puck chasing. Detroit's UAW hockey team still faces off against the Red Wings alumni team every year, with all proceeds from tickets and concessions benefiting the Clark Park sports complex as spectators watch their union brothers take on the Motor City's sporting legends. UAW nights are a regular feature of junior hockey marketing efforts in the region. It's a simple way to draw a big, raucous crowd of hockey fanatics in the middle of any week regardless of the team's position in the league standings. The UAW may have frightened suburban Nashville, but when union members from Michigan, Illinois, Indiana, and Wisconsin moved south in the early 1990s, they brought their beloved game with them.

"When we first came here, people would say, 'Are you with Saturn? This town is going to hell,'" said Mike Herron, chair of UAW Local 1853 in Spring Hill and one of the first GM laborers to work at Saturn. "To these people the word 'union' meant one of two things: General Sherman or Jimmy Hoffa."[2]

The midwestern union members brought families, and the kids brought their sticks and skates and dreams of on-ice glory. The closest rink, Centennial Sportsplex, was up in Nashville, and a traffic-choked I-65 stood between UAW families and valuable ice time. But giving up on the game wasn't an option. Instead, they built an inline hockey rink at the Local 1853 union hall, located alongside the Town Center Parkway, later renamed for former UAW president Stephen P. Yokich. Among a collection of northern transplants lost in a sea of molasses-sweet accents and football mania, the rink served as an anchor for the community. But many Tennesseans did not take kindly to the interlopers' presence and indulgence in a time-honored, distinctly northern sporting pastime.

On July 31, 1990, the first Saturn rolled off the line at the Spring Hill Manufacturing plant. Six months later, Danny and Kelly Geoffrion arrived in Williamson County, their one-year-old son, Blake, sleeping soundly in the back seat of their car.

"They called us hicks with sticks," says Kelly Geoffrion, Blake's mother. The Geoffrions were hockey royalty, not blue-collar shift workers. Money wasn't tight around the Geoffrion household, and there was plenty of room in the family van for fresh new hockey gear. Danny had moved them to Tennessee to work insurance, not weld bumpers onto new Saturns. Still, just the sight of stick blades peeking out of equipment bags was enough to lump them in with That Union Crowd.

In the US South, especially in the 1980s and '90s, the logistics of raising a kid on skates could shake the faith of even the most determined northern transplant. Ice time availability makes or breaks a hockey town, and with Williamson County's perpetually booming real estate market, six-acre land parcels weren't exactly ripe for the picking—and freezing. The inline rink at the UAW hall was only a stopgap; hockey prodigies need to learn the feel of their skates biting into the ice, of a hard dig coast-to-coast as the chips spray from beneath their blades. Yet even in the most unlikely of climates, nothing speeds up the building of ice rinks faster than the arrival of a professional franchise. In 1993, when Minnesota's beloved North Stars moved to Dallas, hockey was an after-thought in North Texas. At the time, the Dallas area (population 3.8 million) had just five rinks, zero high school hockey programs, zero travel teams, and only 250 registered youth players.

Two and a half decades later, fourteen thousand kids in North Texas were registered in youth hockey leagues, and the Dallas metropolitan region was home to more than twenty rinks. In 1990, the same year that the Saturn plant opened its doors and its employment rolls to migrating union members from the Midwest, Centennial Sportsplex opened in Nashville as a catchall recreational facility, with youth hockey only one of a number of interests competing for ice time. The refrig-erated building was located on Twenty-Fifth Avenue, a stone's throw from Vanderbilt University, and it would soon become a home away from home and a respite from the Tennessee heat for the Geoffrions and hundreds of other transplants. Centennial expanded in the late 1990s when the National Hockey League came to town, adding another desperately needed skating venue and doubling as a practice facility for professional players. The four Geoffrion brothers and their fellow rink rats thus had an up-close-and-personal view of professional hockey—or at least of the relatively polished and regulated version of the game endorsed by the NHL. For locals, this was a relief. Until the Predators came to Nashville, pro hockey was not for children's eyes.

∼

The history of professional hockey in the Volunteer State is a checkered one. It's defined by fits and starts and by gaps big enough to drive a

Zamboni through. In 1962, a new franchise brought hockey, in the form of toothless Canadian mercenaries doing battle between the boards for $150 a week, to the baffled football fans of the area. The Nashville Dixie Flyers played in the independent minor professional Eastern Hockey League, home to "some of the toughest and most vicious characters who ever laced up skates"[3] and the inspiration for the iconic hockey movie *Slap Shot*, starring Paul Newman. This was the helmetless era, and the skulls of opposing players were too tempting of a target for the Dixie skaters to pass up. "First thing I learned when I came down is, you take the blade of your stick and you sharpen the toe. Use a rasp, sandpaper, and then when you got close to a guy, you could slap him in the head with it and cut him open,"[4] said Don Graham, winger for the Dixie Flyers from '62 to '64. The fans shared this feeling of violent hostility toward opposing teams. After a hard-fought win against the rival Long Island Ducks, one Dixie Flyers fan pelted a Duck player with trash; the player promptly spun around and launched his stick into the crowd like a javelin, spearing a woman in the head. Players quickly began punching it out on the ice, and police eventually arrived at Nashville's Municipal Auditorium to break up the fighting. The franchise folded in 1971, much to the chagrin of its small but dedicated fan base.

Ten years later, professional minor league hockey returned to Middle Tennessee when the Nashville South Stars, an affiliate of the Minnesota North Stars, took to the ice, but the team lasted only two seasons. Bob Suter, famed member of Miracle on Ice team that took the gold medal at the 1980 Olympics in Lake Placid, New York, briefly laced up his skates with the team before going on to play in the NHL. More than twenty years later, his son Ryan took the same path Blake Geoffrion followed to the NHL: prep hockey at Culver Military Academy; the US National Team Development Program in Ann Arbor, Michigan; the University of Wisconsin Badgers Division I program; and finally pro hockey with the Nashville Predators, where he and Blake celebrated together on the ice after Geoffrion's first NHL goal.

Two more franchises made appearances as Tennessee inched toward an NHL team—the Nashville Knights (1989–96) and the Nashville

Nighthawks/Ice Flyers (1996–98). By the time the sun was setting on the Ice Flyers' final season, Wisconsin businessman Craig Leipold was looking south, and his eyes were set on a bigger, better, and more lucrative version of the sport.

A native of Racine, Wisconsin, Leipold grew up a self-described "really bad hockey player" whose habit of stumbling from one success story to the next became legendary. He quit his job as a salesman at twenty-nine to start a telemarketing business, and by thirty-four he had sold his share of the company for millions. The following year he married Helen Johnson, who appeared on *Forbes* magazine's list of richest Americans. By the mid-1990s, he'd fallen in love with sunny Nashville and had Music City civic leaders walking in lockstep to support his efforts to land a new professional hockey franchise. On January 13, 1997, he found himself across a Midtown Manhattan conference table from NHL commissioner Gary Bettman, Leipold's trademark mullet brushing his collar as he pleaded his case for southern-fried hockey. On June 25, the NHL Board of Governors conditionally granted Leipold Holdings a franchise. Before handing over a check for $80 million, Leipold called the University of Wisconsin's hockey coach, Jeff Sauer, to ask him to explain the finer points of the game.

By the following May, the NHL's newest team was officially headed south. This latest iteration of hockey fandom in Middle Tennessee was in some ways as unconventional as its predecessors. Michigan transplants came to the old Nashville Arena in droves, calling themselves Predawings and displaying their Detroit sports paraphernalia and union cards with pride. And naturally the Geoffrion family was there, Danny and Kelly with their four boys in tow, reveling in the smack of sticks and the crunch of bodies separated from the fans by only half an inch of Plexiglass. The Geoffrions had snapped up season tickets on the cheap and could be found leaning forward from the front row of the third level whenever the Preds didn't interfere with the boys' playing schedules, which wasn't often. But the new team would need more than just lost midwesterners and one family of French-Canadian hockey junkies to keep the lights on and the ice cold at the arena. NASCAR fans came

for the speed; football fans the chance to battle back offseason bore-
dom. Even college hoops fans snapped up partial season ticket packages
to nail down better seats for the Southeastern Conference's men's basketball tournament.

The Predator franchise encountered a deeply uninformed fan base. In
the run-up to the inaugural season, the team paid college kids minimum
wage to hang out at malls and other suburban Nashville watering holes,
pumping up passersby for a game no one understood. Nat Harden was
one of those kids, making seven dollars an hour while trying to hustle
hockey to the Williamson County football faithful. He passed out pam-
phlets that contained a glossary of hockey terms and a rink diagram for
the uninitiated. He tried and failed to sell season tickets. But somehow,
he and his fellow summertime employees steered enough fans to the
rink on the corner of Sixth and Broadway.

At long last, there was live NHL hockey only eleven miles north of
Brentwood, and the Geoffrion family certainly didn't need the Hockey
101 lessons that Predators' broadcasters were offering each week. If anything, the new franchise, wobbling as it took its first few steps into the
world, needed the Geoffrions. The team's front office invited the family
to the official unveiling of the Predators' home and away jerseys at the
brand-new CoolSprings Galleria in Franklin. Not as members of the
crowd, though. When head coach Barry Trotz stepped up to the bank
of microphones to address the local media and a few dozen polite but
bemused suburban Tennesseans, Blake and Sebastian Geoffrion, drowning in oversized jerseys and beaming with wonder, stood on either side.

For Blake and his brothers, the new team validated what they had
always known: hockey was their sport.

Danny Geoffrion, Blake's father, was himself a product of the Canadian
hockey system, a stick-and-puckster just beginning to thaw out after
decades of playing on the frozen waterways and indoor arenas of Quebec
and Ontario. The four seasons and green fairways of Middle Tennessee
represented a chance to play a little golf and maybe, for an instant, to

set aside the chilled intensity of rink life. When he recalls the good old days, Danny's squarish face splits easily with a broad smile, a white crossbar of teeth splashed across his tanned skin. He likes to offer up that smile halfway through the punchline of a good joke, before his listener has even had a chance to chuckle. His Quebecois roots still creep into his voice; boys become *boyz*, do is *doue* and to is *toue*, with the extra vowels stretching.

Sitting at the Thanksgiving table, the former NHL forward recounts for his guests how he first dressed his boys in oversized skates and pads and watched them clomp around, at the same time reassuring them that a life without hockey was OK, too. But no ill-fitting equipment could keep Blake Geoffrion from his athletic birthright. "I remember loving how the gear felt," he said. It was natural, a second skin, a visceral tie to a game that had consumed his family for generations. Even when a whiff of odor from hand-me-down breezers reached his nostrils, the comforting shell of hockey gear assured him that moments later, his skates would be hitting the ice. And that guarantee of freedom, renewed with every second of ice time he could beg or borrow, was intoxicating.

Blake's first forays onto the ice mirrored those of his older brother—pushing a chair around the rink at Centennial Sportsplex as a parent shuffled behind and date-night teenagers tripped past. He was immediately hooked, plunged into the early stages of a lifelong fascination. Everything became about the game. "I remember sitting around the kitchen table, listening to all the stories my dad used to tell us about his playing days. They were funny, they were sad, they were happy—all emotions kind of running through my head." The smell of the arena followed him everywhere: sweat, stale and potent and lingering, burrowed into every thread of cloth bags and leather-lined gloves. But it was more than that: the scent of fresh tape, sticky-sweet coming off the roll; foam, flecking away in little pieces from the inside of a helmet, releasing an almost-industrial smell as it mashed against the plastic shell with every hit and every fall; new laces and used laces and broken, knotted laces spliced one inch at a time, their flat cotton faces soaked and dried repeatedly with the shavings of a thousand practices and games;

and ice—the smooth, clean ice that magically appears behind a Zamboni, its odor lingering heavy in the air. It was the stink of a rink rat. The smell of a hockey player. To Blake, it smelled like home.

His mother lost track of him one day, and when she found him, Blake was riding his tricycle around the driveway, circling again and again, starting in small laps, a little wider with each pass. Kelly chuckled at his furrowed brow, the intensity of concentration etched across his three-year-old face.

"What are you doing out here, Blake?"

"This is called a 'boni, Momma," he replied. "I'm cleaning the ice. Get off of it!"

Danny was determined that his son would become a solid technical skater, given that neither he nor his father, Boom Boom, had ever won praise for the way they navigated the ice. Fortunately for Blake, skating grace was woven into his genes, too. His grandmother had been a champion figure skater, and her abilities inspired Danny to sign his son up for individual lessons with a local figure skating coach. Like a boxer taking dance classes for improved footwork, Blake built a foundation early on, rejecting wasted motion and harnessing his strength. Put a stick in his hands and point him toward a goal, and the boy could really fly.

The first time Danny had glanced toward the bench to see his own father standing there, coach's clipboard in hand, the eyes of a dozen reporters had followed his gaze. The two had never shared the juice-box innocence of youth hockey. No, Danny's father had missed all that. He was always too busy—too busy setting records and hoisting the Stanley Cup, season after season, for the Montreal Canadiens. Danny would come home from Pee Wee games flushed with his success, only to find his father staring sternly back at him from the sports page, his famous features frozen in black and white.

In 1968, the year Danny turned ten, the elder Geoffrion finally retired. Joseph Bernard André Geoffrion, known as Bernie or Boom Boom to most, had won six Stanley Cups playing for the hometown Canadiens—

three before Danny's birth, three after. Over eighteen seasons, he had won the Calder Trophy as rookie of the year and the Art Ross Trophy as the league's leading scorer, had led the NHL in game-winning goals three times, and had become only the second player ever to score fifty goals in a season, all while wielding the booming slap shot that had earned him his nickname.

A man like that didn't just hang up his skates and turn to scrapbook-ing to pass the time. He accepted his first head coaching job with the New York Rangers weeks after announcing his retirement from playing and was bound for the States just as soon as his visa paperwork cleared. When health problems forced him to resign midseason, he returned to Canada, but Danny was soon off to pursue his own serious hockey career, living with a billet family in Cornwall, Ontario, and doing his best to drown out the whispers with the blast of goal horns. *He's good, but he'll never be like his father.*

With 143 points in seventy-one games for the Cornwall Royals of the Quebec Major Junior Hockey League, his efforts seemed to be work-ing. The Canadiens agreed. Montreal drafted him in the first round, eighth overall, in the 1978 draft. It was a rare idyllic moment for father and son, a moment of pride shared at the old Queen Elizabeth Hotel.

The Habs called Boom Boom a week before Danny's first season with the team. Scotty Bowman, who had coached the team to four consecu-tive Stanley Cup championships, was leaving, and they wanted old No. 5 to take over as coach. Boom Boom had never doubted himself, never apologized to anyone in his quest for sporting immortality, and here was the moment to secure his canonization, to lead his beloved Habs to a fifth win in five years, the first ever player turned coach to claim a championship for Montreal.

Requesting permission was an alien concept to Bernie, but he made the call anyway. If his son asked him to, he would take a pass on the coaching job of a lifetime.

When Boom Boom asked the question, he heard a pause and then a chuckle. Of course Danny wanted him to take the gig. What else could a son say to that question?

The two passed the next eight weeks in relative silence. Aside from whistle tweets and grunted instructions in practices and games, the famous father and the son saddled with impossible expectations hardly spoke. It was the most consistent time the two had spent together since Danny's birth, yet neither could find the words to fit the moment, to fill the air. Each spoke constantly, blessed with stereotypical French-Canadian loquacity, to everyone else. But "in the Montreal Forum, on the buses, in the airports, in the hotels, they would walk past each other as strangers," reported the Associated Press.

Boom Boom was especially sensitive to any criticism that he was playing his son too much, a worry for all fathers turned coaches but especially for one taking the helm of the reigning Stanley Cup champions. He knew his boy was good, even if he had rarely seen Danny play. But Boom Boom was also trapped, caught between the expectations of a fan base that had grown accustomed to winning, a front office that didn't yet trust him, and a chilly family dynamic that haunted him on the ice and off.

The new coach was focused on winning, and Danny was focused mostly on reassuring the rest of the team that he was just one of the guys—a locker room chatterbox always good for a laugh and definitely not a liability who might go running and tattle to his daddy. His good humor and gregariousness served him well, and soon he had even the most skeptical veterans convinced he was *one of zee boyz.* There was just one problem: Danny seemed to have forgotten how to score.

Questions from the media grew more pointed as one game after another passed without a Geoffrion goal. The rumblings from the fan base grew louder, too, since the fans were unaccustomed to keeping their opinions to themselves. As if the presence of an uncommunicative father and the weight of an entire province's presuppositions weren't enough burdens for the young player, the Habs were struggling to win, at least at the pace that would make the Drive for Five something more than just a marketing slogan.

Montreal lost to the New York Islanders on December 11, 1979, the squad's sixth road game without a victory. Four days later, Boom Boom resigned his dream job. He refused to wait around and be fired just to collect the severance he didn't feel he had earned. His stomach ulcers were back, causing excruciating internal bleeding. The pressure, the losing, had become both physically and emotionally unbearable. He would be relegated to watching his son from the stands for the rest of the season.

~

Danny should have been sent down to Halifax for some minor league confidence building right then. Instead, being both the heir to the Geoffrion throne and a first-round draft pick with an exorbitant contract, he was relegated to a fifth-line winger role, his playing time dwindling to almost nothing, homeless on his hometown team. At the end of the season, Montreal left him unprotected, and he was picked up by the fledgling Winnipeg Jets. In another year, he would leave the NHL for good.

Bernie "Boom Boom" Geoffrion was inducted into the Hockey Hall of Fame in 1972, and the Canadiens retired his number in 2006. In 2017, he was named one of the one hundred greatest players in the history of the NHL.

And his son? Danny went on to become the greatest beer league hockey player Middle Tennessee had ever seen. He still plays every Wednesday morning and sometimes on the weekends.

~

"Remember," Danny always reminded Blake, "just because you're a Geoffrion doesn't mean you have to play hockey." OK, Dad. Sure.

And so, as a line of Ford Explorers made its way down to the football fields of Brentwood for the start to the fall season, the Geoffrions were bound for the ranks of the Nashville Youth Hockey League (NYHL) and every patch of open ice they could find. The first Geoffrion brother had hit the rink in an NYHL sweater in 1991. By the late '90s, all four were spending every possible moment on the ice, sharing the rink with a ragtag collection of teammates and opponents, disgruntled castaways of the gridiron and the basketball court. Danny, now donning a coach's

Blake (*front row, far right*), Coach Danny (*top right*), and members
pose for a Nashville Youth Hockey League team photo, 1992.
Photograph by Kelly Geoffrion, 1992.

whistle and lanyard, brought a fierce competitiveness to his new role as
coach of Blake's Mites team. "Now, just because you all made the team
last year doesn't mean you're going to make the team this year. This is
serious stuff. If you don't like it, find another league." His Quebecois
growl hung in the air, a breath-stealing soliloquy for the huddle of eight-
year-olds at center ice. "But Dad," piped up Blake, coasting into the
middle of the group, "there are only twelve of us."

"Congratulations, you've all made the team!"

Blake's blossoming obsession with the family game wasn't well received
by everyone. Ken and Marie lived next door to the Geoffrions in Brentwood, nice old folks who never bothered anyone. Ken was retired, but
Marie still worked at Dillard's department store, selling high-end clothes

to high-end ladies. She wasn't around much, and Kelly made a point to check in on Ken from time to time, bringing him food, warning him when the weather was acting up, sending Danny over to cut his lawn when the summers got too hot. In that distinct southern fashion, they were friendly even if they weren't quite friends.

One day, Kelly ran into Ken in the yard, and he announced matter-of-factly that he and Marie were "goin' into the assisted livin'." Kelly assured him that they would be missed and hugged him goodbye, and they turned back to their respective houses. Later that evening, she heard a knock.

"Well, hey, Marie," she said with a smile after opening the door, a bit surprised.

"I just wanted you to know that Ken and I are moving," her neighbor answered curtly.

"I heard, and we're happy for you, but we're sure going to miss you," replied Kelly.

"And I just wanted you to know," Marie said, charging ahead, "that you were the worst neighbors anybody ever had. We could never sit in our backyard and enjoy it without worrying about being killed by a hockey puck."

Kelly paused, her smile frozen in shock. Then she turned her head and called back into the house, "Danny, this woman's got something she wants to say to you!"

Travel hockey became all-consuming as soon as the boys hit the age of seven. Blake and his three brothers would play a dozen combined games some weekends; Kelly would take one boy, Danny the other, and the other two would leg it out with teammates back in Nashville. The inside of the family minivan became scarred with stick marks as groaning bags of pads and skates and helmets and gloves ("Don't forget the socks! Did you get the socks? For everyone?!") were loaded and unloaded in transit from one tournament to the next. The back seat was home not only to the usual sibling bickering but also to the priceless hockey education that only crisscrossing the South with a former pro can bring. Old stories about pond hockey, about playing juniors and living in a billet home in Ontario, about their grandfather, their great-grandfather, the beauty of a game that combined speed and grace with strength and intensity and nonstop action—all of it seeped into the minds of the Geoffrion brothers as the odometer ticked off miles. Another chance to strap on skates and chase rink-side immortality awaited the boys at the end of each drive. The Southern Youth Hockey League was spread out across the region—Nashville, Memphis, and Atlanta as well as Huntsville, Alabama, where tryouts were held for the Southeastern USA Hockey regional team every year. When Blake was selected for that team, he got his first shot at facing real competition, playing against rival regional teams from New England, the Northern Plains, the Rocky Mountains, the West, and elsewhere. Minnesota, Michigan, and Massachusetts were each classified as a separate district.

Those northern kids were good. They could move, they hit hard, controlled loose pucks, and finished set plays with a finesse that dazzled their southern competitors. And yet Blake, surprising no one, skated right along with them. Travel teams became the showcase for his hockey sense, something for which many pray but only a few select players truly possess. "Compared to all the other players, he was a notch above," recounted Danny. "As soon as Blake started playing travel hockey, he stood out. I've been around long enough that I was able to tell, he's definitely got it. But even at an early age, he was dominant."

Hockey sense is an ill-defined but universally understood concept. It's an aptitude for seeing the ice and reacting to changes in the game even before they happen. Find the open ice with eyes, feet, stick. Reach it, then keep moving, cycle the puck to another open patch where teammates will appear as if by magic. Split the defenders, leave enough room to spin, shift the stick from hand to hand as motion drives the play, and *bam!* hit that netting with authority. To see any kid do it is special. To see a southern kid do it was extraordinary.

Hockey dominated the television before bed and the conversation at breakfast. Danny wasn't particular about watching a single team, so the boys could bask in the aura of the NHL superstars of their choice. Mike Modano was a favorite of Blake's, a left winger who moved with the North Stars from Minnesota to Dallas and inspired thousands of southern youngsters to pick up sticks and pester their parents for rides to the rink. Steve Yzerman was another, a lifelong Detroit Red Wing forever known as the Captain in Michigan dive bars and now recognized as one of the greatest players of all time. The players on TV, contemporary and cool, seemed so distant from the historical hockey figures of his father's retelling.

Yzerman's brilliance in the 1996 playoffs seared itself into young Blake's mind. How could anyone forget it? Game 7 of the Eastern Conference Semifinals, Detroit versus St. Louis, and the two teams had been smashing each other around the rink for an eternity, the last gasp of enmity after a season of mutual hatred. Yzerman, like everyone else, was on his last legs, but he never showed it. As both teams changed lines yet again, putting fresh players on the ice, Blues center Wayne Gretzky heeled the puck and lost it in the neutral zone, and the Captain picked it up and raced along the boards with a speed belying the two OT lights illuminated on the scoreboard. He reared back at the blue line, more than sixty feet from the net, and laid down a slap shot *and the puck goes in!* Joe Louis Arena erupted, air horns blaring as players piled on top of Yzerman, their leader and hero. The hockey world went wild. At the Geoffrion house, pandemonium reigned. For an eight-year-old with stars in his eyes, it was enough inspiration to last a lifetime.

Hockey heroes didn't just live on television, though. Blake's grandfather, his Pappy, would come to visit, never volunteering his stories in self-aggrandizing fashion but always willing to share his hockey knowledge with four wide-eyed grandsons who watched rapturously as the inventor of the slap shot put holes in their backyard fence. Danny watched the demolition of his fence, too, although with a little more chagrin than wonder.

Blake loved to play. The feeling of shooting pucks was so satisfying, and he loved to imitate his grandfather, that slap shot, giggling at the gratification of a puck struck just right. He didn't really make the connection between the games he played in the backyard and the games playing out across the living room television. Pappy wasn't Mario Lemieux. He wasn't *cool*. He was just . . . Pappy.

Winters were for organized hockey—endless practices and games, each year more competitive than the last—and summers were for street games, as one unlucky brother got stuck in the net and the others played two-on-one across the asphalt driveway, oblivious to the parade of Brentwood's uninitiated who rolled past and gawked, open-mouthed, at these stick-wielding maniacs. This was the seasonal inverse of the nonstop pickup games on the frozen ponds of Montreal. It also wasn't much of a setting for honing budding stars. "In the North, you know, my dad said, he and his buddies would always get together and have really great games. Well, I'd get together with my buddies and they all sucked. They didn't know what hockey was," said Blake.

Hockey is a sport cursed by comparisons. It remains the little brother of major North American sports, even after the miracle in Lake Placid when a group of college kids defeated the mighty Soviets became the greatest moment in US sports history. Around the average sports bar high-top, Wayne Gretzky is still "Michael Jordan on skates," the Montreal Canadiens are basically "like the Yankees," and Steve Yzerman's late-game heroics are "hockey's version of the Catch."

Most puck heads considered the comparisons game a regretful, irreverent burden. For a storied hockey family forced to navigate southern society, though, comparisons could come in handy. Trying to tell the kids at school that Blake's granddad, Howie Morenz, had been a three-time Hart Trophy winner and an original inductee into the Hockey Hall of Fame would, more likely than not, elicit a "Well isn't that nice, sweetie" response in Williamson County. But describing Morenz as the Babe Ruth of Hockey would cause the ears of even the most ardently traditional Tennesseans to perk up with interest. Now they understood.

Howard Morenz never finished high school. He followed his father and his brother into the Grand Trunk Railway power shops, apprenticing as a machinist in the grime of 1920s industrial Ontario. Morenz took a workingman's pride in his tradesman status, even if he refused to dress the part. His distinct high boots earned him daily harassment from the other boys in the railway shop. When needled about them, Morenz just shrugged and shyly smiled: "I've got a valuable pair of ankles to protect."

The Montreal Canadiens appreciated a well-turned ankle, and Howie's set soon caught their attention, as did his play for the Railway's apprentice teams and the junior squads of Mitchell and Stratford. On July 7, 1923, he signed his first professional contract, and the Stratford Streak immediately began to carve a place for himself in the record books as well as in the hearts of the Habs faithful. He wasn't Quebecois, but he was blue-collar in a way that Montrealers could understand and respect.

"To the millworkers and tram drivers and off-duty cabbies who jammed the rush end of the Forum in Montreal and called themselves the Millionaires, Morenz was a superhuman figure," wrote Trent Frayne for *Maclean's* in 1953. "Between periods they toasted him surreptitiously in homemade gin. Their battle cry, 'Les Canadiens sont là!' never reached such frenzy as when Morenz started winding up behind his own net with a queer little bouncing jig that sent him hurtling down the ice in an exhilarating moment of excitement that reached its crescendo when he threw himself between the defensemen and crashed the puck past the goalkeeper."

Over the next thirteen years, Morenz would revolutionize the game. He played the first six years of his NHL career at a time when forward passes were banned, making his one-man rushes an explosive gambit unmatched across the league. Observers declared him hockey's first superstar.

"Morenz was one of the greatest back-checkers I ever saw," remembered Toe Blake, who won a record eight Stanley Cups as the longtime Canadiens coach to go with the three he had previously won as a player. Morenz was a five-foot, nine-inch whirling dervish in an era of limited offense, a futuristic forward happy to embarrass defenders with his speed and to score and score again en route to winning three Art Ross Trophies for leading the league in points.

On January 28, 1937, Howie was battling with Chicago's Earl Siebert, a hulking defenseman thirty pounds heavier than Morenz, when he slipped and slid feet first into the dasher at the base of the boards. He raised his leg to brace against the impact, and his skate blade stuck firmly into the wood. Siebert crashed into him from behind, and the leg shattered, breaking in four places. "Don't count me out yet," he told reporters from his hospital bed. Hockey fans above the border and below prayed for his recovery; bags stuffed with mail from well-wishers piled up at the hospital. But Morenz slowly came to the realization that his playing days were over. He refused food and lay in his bed, sleepless, night after night, deteriorating in body and mind. On March 8, 1937, the great athlete slipped and fell. Doctors found his body motionless on the floor. He had died of a coronary embolism, but Habs fans always believed that he died of a broken heart.

Three days later, his body lay in a prince's coffin at center ice in the Forum. Thousands of fans filed past his casket, watched over by an honor guard of four Canadiens teammates. Even after his death, that day would live on, swelling with significance in the memories of generations of Habs fans. A flower arrangement in the shape of the number 7 rested atop the polished wood, a note from his three children tucked within the buds and leaves. Tributes rang out in Boston and New York and across Canada, with funeral wreaths laid by friends and foes alike. The prime minister honored Morenz by authorizing the playing of "The Last Post," the bugler's call traditionally sounded for lives lost on the battlefield, the same chilling notes that had rung out so often through the devastation of the Great War that had ended so many Canadian lives.

On November 2, 1937, the Canadiens retired Morenz's No. 7. He would remain alone in the rafters, holding eternal watch over the battles fought below, until Maurice Richard's No. 9 joined him in 1961.

Family was the bedrock of the Geoffrion game, and hockey heroes haunted the halls of their home. Look backward for inspiration, look around you for someone to play against. Look ahead—maybe—for your own shot at greatness.

~

In a fledgling market like Nashville, enthusiasm could carry Blake and his brothers only so far. Growth and success demanded a high level of competition, and the good players lived north of the Mason-Dixon— in Cicero, Pontiac, Janesville, Hershey, Winthrop. To get exposure—to scouts, coaches, athletic directors, and big-time programs that offered a pathway to the NHL—teenagers loaded their gear, said goodbye to their parents, and got on a bus heading up I-65. Once they realized that their hockey futures, if any, were to be found in the brisk winters and stiff competition of the North and the Midwest, the serious players never came back. "The juniors" are hockey's equivalent of baseball's travel team system, though in some ways more professionalized. Competing leagues have teams scattered across the United States and Canada, systematically scooping up promising youngsters beginning at age sixteen. Players live with host families, often for several years at a time, and travel thousands of miles to play against elite opponents across North America and increasingly Northern and Eastern Europe. Those who don't go the junior hockey route can choose prep school hockey instead: Choate Rosemary in Connecticut and Kimball Union in New Hampshire draw the best young skaters from the Northeast, while Shattuck St. Mary's and Culver Military Academy lock up many of the finest midwestern prospects.

As Nashville teams entered tournaments in Chicago, Detroit, Minneapolis, and Boston, scouts quickly moved to grab the very best. The talent drain was real. And Blake Geoffrion, the torchbearer for youth hockey in Williamson County and the greater Nashville area, was at the vanguard. Coach Al Clark and wellness director Dan Davidge of the Culver Military Academy had recognized the South as an untapped market. In the summer of 2000, as the sun beat down on muggy Huntsville, Davidge stood disappointedly watching the USA Hockey Southeastern tryouts unfold in front of him. He'd harbored high hopes for the long drive south, cranking up the air conditioner and ignoring the Confederate flags whipping from antennas as he searched for the next great US skater. But the kids he'd come to see didn't have it. So to kill time, he sauntered over to see the seventh graders next door, ripping clumsily up and down the ice in a one-on-one drill. Only one caught his eye—a tall, lanky kid who stood head and shoulders above his peers. He wasn't the greatest skater, tripping over his feet as his elbows and knees lagged slightly behind his hands and feet. But every time he came down the ice, he scored! Davidge watched, flabbergasted, as the kid beat the defender three, four, five, six, seven times, scoring with ease. Those hands drew his gaze. Nice hands, attached to long arms and shoulders with room to grow.

Davidge turned to a parent sitting beside him: "Who's the big kid, the one who can't stop scoring?"

"That's Geoffrion!"

To a guy who had grown up along the Grand River in Dunnville, Ontario, these were magic words. Davidge quickly found Danny, introduced himself, and asked if the family was any relation to Boom Boom. After more than a decade spent rink-side in the South, Danny still wasn't used to people with any sort of hockey knowledge creeping out of the humid shadows in places like Huntsville. "Whadya know about Boom Boom?" Davidge was quick to roll out his Canadian credentials, and the two Canucks hit it off, talking hockey and long winters and the misplaced bravado of football fans in their adopted country.

Over the next few years, Danny helped coach at the summer hockey clinics Culver hosted in Nashville, always talking with Davidge about the academy, its hockey program, its academics, and just as important, the path it offered to Division I hockey and a college scholarship. The family was nuts about education. When Boom Boom came to town, he would harp on the need for a college degree, recognizing early the twenty-first century's demand for more advanced and formal schooling than he'd received.

A letter bearing the crimson Culver logo came in the mailbox not long after Blake's fourteenth birthday. He'd grown quickly that year—Danny always said that Blake was lucky to get his height early—and his play in the USA Hockey tournaments, combined with the raw ability so evident at Culver's hockey clinics, had deepened the Davidge's impression from that first Alabama afternoon. Two Culver alumni names had already been etched on the Stanley Cup's silver-and-nickel face, and the school's hockey bona fides were well established. Fortunately for Blake, a couple of Nashville-area players had already made the trek north and spoke glowingly of the Culver experience. And so did their mothers. Hockey moms talk, and Kelly Geoffrion had always been hesitant about the idea of junior hockey and billet homes. Danny had left home at the age of thirteen, and Kelly swore that her boys would not do the same. It tore her up to imagine an empty chair at her kitchen table, and it hurt even more to think of other moms asking why he was "sent away." Did he do something wrong?

But Blake badly wanted to go, so Kelly consented. In the fall of 2002, he headed to Culver, on the banks of Indiana's Lake Maxinkuckee. He would leave, two years later, with more of an education than he could have bargained for.

Culver Military Academy wasn't simply a breeding ground for elite athletes. Founded in 1894, the institution prided itself on its military rigidity and strict adherence to discipline. Morning roll call was at 7:00 a.m. sharp; boots were to be shined and polished, uniforms pressed and neat, quarters tidy, and facial hair nonexistent. The last requirement wasn't a problem for many of the fresh-faced teens who showed up for lessons in character, leadership, and athletic excellence, but for most of the boys, the other aspects of their new life constituted a dramatic shift from the comfortable home lives they had left behind.

"It was miserable," said Blake. "I was a young kid, and my mom used to do all my laundry, dishes. Now I had to essentially live on my own while going through emotional, physical, and mental changes." or "tac" officers expected each young charge to make his bed so tightly that a quarter bounced off of it would spring back into one's hand. No dust was permitted, no fingerprints on glass or dirt on floors. When Blake failed his room inspection for the first time, he spent hours the next night scrubbing the place clean, making and remaking the bed, disgusted and embarrassed. He stood nearly shivering at attention the following morning, eyes fixed forward as his tac officer spat out a verdict: "Well, Geoffrion, you passed." Always the relentless competitor, Blake leapt into the air and whooped, pumping his fist, nearly knocking himself out on the ceiling beam. So much for military decorum.

Some of the older players gave him the cold shoulder—postgrads still playing for the varsity team at eighteen, nineteen, even twenty years old who were threatened by the highly touted southern star or disdainful of his determination to play on the varsity squad, the A team, as a freshman. Blake wanted to fit in socially, always eager to please. Too eager. It didn't work well at Culver. His fellow cadets knew the drill; showed up smartly clad in dark gray jackets, overseas caps, and polished black dress shoes; and fit seamlessly into the complex system of promotions, demerits, punishment, and privilege that rules the life of a boarding school enrollee. One instructor, a steely eyed Vietnam combat veteran, was especially keen on Blake as a target for discipline, or at least it seemed that way to the wet-behind-the-ears freshman. And just when cadets got a free moment, when the endless series of drills and chores—interspersed with orders barked into their ears from inches away—eased up for the briefest instant, an academic workload came down to crush even a savvy and well-prepared student's spirit.

Applicants were warned that Culver's academic standards were tougher than those of many colleges. The classes were demanding and accompanied by a relentless homework regimen that allowed no coasting, even for the academy's star athletes. Culver proudly described its "Learning to Learn" program as "building skills of understanding through rigorous challenges." In true Culver fashion, it was a brutally honest assessment. There would be no hiding in plain sight for Blake or his teammates. Hockey stars and bookworms alike spent the waning moments of class frantically scribbling notes in anticipation of the next test before seizing their books and bags at the sound of the bell and sprinting across campus. For the players, their destination was the academy's Henderson Ice Arena, home to an NHL-sized rink and a larger Olympic-sized one—as much rink room as the entire Nashville area offered to its collection of youth league, beer league, and high school hockey teams combined.

The hour between 3:15 p.m., when the last bell rang, and 4:15 p.m., when the first whistle blew for practice, was a magical one. It was a time for locker-room camaraderie—practical jokes and loud music and endless ribbing about the cute girls and failed tests and bodily functions that define the world of any teenaged boy, even a hockey prodigy.

At least four days a week, ninety-minute practices left Blake dripping with sweat, shaking his head at the first real on-ice adversity he had faced. He'd come into the academy with sky-high expectations, a lanky boy wonder with a sterling hockey pedigree. The scrutiny was more intense than he'd ever experienced, but greater than the pressure from his coaches or counselors was the burden Blake placed on himself.

To perform on the ice.

To be liked by his teammates.

To fulfill the expectations he'd been carrying since he'd first grasped a hockey stick and had seen the Geoffrion name sewn on the back of his jersey.

It was too much for a fourteen-year-old to handle. He took all criticism personally, finding a corner and ripping the ice to shreds as he worked to improve his skating with a frantic determination.

But it wasn't enough.

For the most part, his gangly teenage body couldn't keep up, and his coaches frequently compared him to Bambi—wobbly kneed, unsteady, unresponsive to the brilliant hockey mind that strained so desperately to force its will on those recalcitrant limbs. He wore holes through his socks just trying to keep up. By December, he'd been demoted to Culver's B team.

The hockey frustrations, the rigorous academics, the spittle from a drill sergeant spraying everywhere in another public dressing down— they were too much to handle. Blake, fed up and ready to quit, finally called home. And so Danny climbed into his red Ford Excursion and began the 417-mile drive north to Culver. As he pulled up, Blake stood outside his dormitory, waiting, a mountain of hockey gear and duffels filled with neatly folded uniforms next to him. He'd had enough. There were better things for him than early morning reveille and B team hockey.

Blake had played a few tournaments with the AAA Cleveland Barons, and they would be happy to have their visiting stud back full time. Danny's Ford ate up asphalt one mile at a time, creeping along the Michigan state line and the south shore of Lake Erie as father and son drove along, mostly in silence. There wasn't much to say. They'd covered thousands of miles along similar routes in the past, always with a hockey game and a higher level of competition waiting at the end of the road. Why should this time be any different? *Quitting* wasn't a word for sporting professionals. It was just a romantic notion that failed to fit into the methodical climb of a future hockey star through the ranks of one of the toughest systems in youth sports. If Cleveland offered more opportunities for ice time and fewer requirements for morning drill and shined shoes, then Blake might as well go east.

They never made it to Cleveland.

"Dad, I think we need to go back," mumbled Blake.

Something in him had changed. Walking away had made him realize how much he had grown, and in a moment of clarity, he recognized an even greater truth: his sense of self had evolved in the face of the rigors of Culver. He had been shown a path to character, to life, that was bigger than the game of hockey.

It was obvious to both father and son that despite all of Culver's demands, leaving had been a mistake, and Danny was willing to gas up and retrace their path along I-90—with one caveat: Blake had to tell Davidge, who had recruited him to come to the academy, that he had changed his mind. So once again Danny was behind the wheel, the tires of the Ford squeaking against the icy asphalt. Another three hundred miles to go, and then an early morning inspection after Blake's humble reentry into the corps of cadets. And Davidge, who assured Blake that his bunk and his locker were still there for him, was impressed with the maturity and courage needed to admit such a lifechanging mistake at so young an age.

Blake turned a corner after that experience, returning to Culver with a renewed determination to embrace the academy's values in all aspects of life: learning to lead, leading to serve, always by example.

By the end of the season, he'd been moved up to the A team, where he was lighting the lamp with one goal after another, affirming his coach's wisdom behind the promotion. His skating was lighter and faster, evincing a new comfort with his body and his play, and by the time the season ended, Blake was riding high. The spring semester flashed by in an instant, and before he knew it, Blake was back in Nashville, once again powering through shifts for USA Hockey's Southeastern team while eagerly anticipating his return to Culver. For the hockey prodigy, things were finally falling into place. By the time he suited up for the academy again in the fall, he was a different player and a different young man, more comfortable in his own skin, higher in rank, surer of the skills he was honing and his place in the Culver hierarchy. His coaches knew him better, too. They'd lived with him for more than a year, watched him mature and thrive and seethe under criticism. Rather than lashing out like other hotheaded teenagers, however, he would turn inward, burying their critiques deep, where they simmered until he needed something extra for the final rep on the bench press, the final shift in a long practice, the final yard to be gained as he muscled an armored truck across a field. Davidge had talked to him about the USA Hockey's National Team Development Program and told the boy he wasn't anywhere close to ready. "Blake, you're an average Midget hockey player," Davidge told him one day. "How do you expect to go to the next level?" It was like someone had flipped a switch, suggesting that his recent gains might only be a faint glimmer of his potential. He was even better the next shift—skating harder, hitting harder—and the next, and the next. Blake's Pappy, Boom Boom, often visited the beautiful Culver campus, hunkering down with Danny and Kelly and Davidge and his wife over a few adult beverages and tales of Canadian days gone by. Eyes bright and voice grizzled, the Geoffrion patriarch always spoke the same conclusion: "My grandson should be going here for free."

Blake, wearing the uniform of a Culver Academy cadet,
speaks with his grandfather, Bernie "Boom Boom" Geoffrion, 2003.
Photograph by Kelly Geoffrion, 2003.

Blake ended his second year as one of the team's top scorers, his soft hands adroitly sending pucks past opposing goaltenders like he was cracking a bullwhip. "It was pure joy," he recalled, and his game reflected it. Blake was starting to view himself in a new light, as was the rest of hockeydom. The annual USA Hockey summer tournaments were packed with scouts hunched over clipboards to shelter their notes from the prying eyes of the zealous parents who shared the bleachers. By the summer of 2004, however, the scouts had no need to shield their pencil scratchings. Everyone knew the three-syllable name that scouts couldn't stop whispering: Geoff-Ree-Awn.

When Blake returned home that summer, he was astonished to find that many of his buddies were swapping the basketball court for the hockey rink. A-Game, a new hockey rink built in Franklin in 2001, was packed for the Centennial-Brentwood game, and Blake watched with surprise as his old friends skated and passed up and down the ice. The hardscrabble sport better suited to the glacial countryside of the Minnesota prairies or the puck-scarred arena boards of Charlestown, Massachusetts, had found a home in this bastion of southern propriety. The arrival of the Nashville Predators brought an aura of respectability to the game, sufficiently removing it from the sordid history of the city's earlier goonish franchises and their equally goonish fans.

Ironically, the dearth of ice in Greater Nashville eventually turned hockey into one of the area's elite sports. The sport's growing aura of exclusivity is hardly unique to Middle Tennessee. In traditional and nontraditional markets alike, lower-income players have been squeezed out of the sport by the rising demand for high-caliber opponents and the costly travel required to reach them as well as by a decline in the amount of available ice time as private skating coaches ren out rinks once open to all. The problem is more pronounced in warmer climates, where all hockey is played indoors, rinks remain scarce, and the drive time to practices and tournaments requires flexible work schedules seldom enjoyed by those outside of the white-collar upper-middle class. "My son will only be as good as I can afford for him to be," said one Nashville hockey parent.

Yet this creeping elitism offers a familiar comfort to those suburban Nashville families who had little interest in the egalitarian version of the sport when it first arrived in Tennessee. The game expanded beyond Yankee transplants and union members, drawing in southern corporate types. Pinstriped suits began replacing work shirts in the bleachers, and the number of Escalades in the parking lots rose each season. "If you look at where most of the travel kids come from, historically you've had an inordinate number come from Hendersonville, which is a very affluent community, and Brentwood in Williamson County, which is a very affluent community," said Kevin Hagan, president of the Greater Nashville Association of Scholastic Hockey. "You don't see a lot of players coming from Davidson County," a more socioeconomically mixed area.

By the middle of the first decade of the twenty-first century, Middle Tennessee had begun to remake hockey in its own image.

Today, the game is a staple in the Volunteer State. USA Hockey has more than twenty-four hundred registered players there, and ice time is reserved for nineteen hours per day at the Centennial Sportsplex in Nashville. Between 2016 and 2021 (with the exception of the COVID-limited 2020 season), the Predators sold out 192 consecutive home games at the renamed Bridgestone Arena, where fans throw catfish onto the ice in a southern iteration of Detroit's octopus-launching tradition.

The state lags far behind the hockey strongholds of Massachusetts, Michigan, and Minnesota, each of which regularly suits up forty thousand burgeoning young superstars every year and vies fiercely—if unofficially—to put the most youth players on the ice. Still, one Tennessee youth hockey team has already snatched a USA Hockey national championship trophy from its northern neighbors. Perani's Hockey World, headquartered in Flint, Michigan, (The Toy Store for the Hockey Player) has opened up a warehouse store in Antioch, Tennessee, east of Brentwood, where local players can get outfitted from head to toe in all manner of shiny new equipment. Profiles of Midget-leaguers and NHLers alike occasionally force college football stories below the fold of the sports section of the *Nashville Tennessean*. Even the country club regulars of Williamson County quietly admit that they wouldn't mind seeing the sport grow—as long as the fairways get their regular mowing.

chapter 2

USA HOCKEY

Gloves and sticks scatter across the ice as five men throw themselves at one another, full tilt and reckless. One skater slips, and others pile on top, thumping his back and head and chest with bare fists. Even the goalie joins the fray, his massive pads cushioning the impact as he barrels into the scrum. And yet no whistle is blown. No referee comes skating in to break up the melee. The crowd noise has reached a fever pitch, people screaming and stomping not in anger but in glee and disbelief.

"Do you believe in miracles? Yes!" The voice of Al Michaels, ABC's play-by-play announcer, pumps through the speakers, relaying the ecstasy to millions of television sets and car radios across the nation. Team USA had beaten the Soviets in a game that instantly became known as the Miracle on Ice, in the semifinals of the 1980 Winter Olympics, the greatest moment in the history of US sports. Two days later, they went on to beat Finland and win the gold medal.

On this night in the tiny village of Lake Placid, New York, the impossible has happened, inspiring a nation locked in a crisis of confidence and a seemingly endless Cold War. A group of unpaid, overworked, able-but-untested college kids beat the unbeatable Soviets, launching themselves into the pantheon of sporting lore. Kids with bright eyes and dull skates raced to their local ponds and rinks the next day, replicating Mark Johnson's stick-side equalizer, Mike Eruzione's timeless and lead-changing wrister. Mark, Mike, and their righteous brothers weren't just trendsetters.

They were heroes.

∾

Fifteen years later, US amateur hockey was in the dumps. The 1980 Olympic gold medal should have been a seminal moment for hockey in the United States, inspiring a generation of new players and bringing parity to the top-heavy hockey culture on the North American continent. Instead, the US success increasingly seemed to be an anomaly, a momentary though glorious peek into a parallel universe where contention for Olympic gold is the norm. "If Canada is hockey's enduring home, U.S. hockey had been a Potemkin village, a facade constructed from the surprising American triumph in the 1960 Olympics and the 1980 Miracle on Ice," wrote sports journalist Michael Farber. The Canadians didn't mind one bit.

The Olympic Games had always been strictly—religiously—amateur. Athletes could not compete if they had ever received any sum of money to compete in any sport. From the lighting of the torch at the first modern Games in 1896, no exception had ever been made.

But everyone has a price, and in 1992, a year after the fall of communism and the triumph of US-led capitalism, the International Olympic Committee finally caved to the pressure of the almighty dollar. An exception to the amateur rule was first made for basketball, and at the '92 Barcelona Games, the Dream Team of US NBA players steamrolled the competition, easily capturing gold. USA Basketball annual revenues reached $100 million once professional stars broke the Olympic amateur barrier. Four years later, NBA annual merchandise sales worldwide topped $3 billion. The NHL owners had seen enough. They wanted their taste, too, and were more than happy to support the inclusion of professional players in the Winter Olympics. On September 30, 1995, the NHL Board of Governors voted to allow professional players to lace up for their home country teams in 1998. At USA Hockey headquarters in Colorado Springs, the alarm bells began to clang.

"There were more pro players from the province of Ontario than from the entire United States at that time," said Ken Martel, the assistant coach for the Michigan Tech men's hockey team. If Team USA wasn't going to just compete but win, officials would need to build a new pipeline all the way from the youth leagues to the NHL. Canada had made a long-term investment in player development, a commitment to cultivation that had filled trophy cases with hardware and Canadian hearts with pride. When Canadian national teams failed to win, coaches and executives were summoned to Parliament not just to answer for their losses but to find answers in time for the next international tournament. When the Olympics announced that professional players would be welcome, Canadians nodded happily, if a bit smugly, while their US counterparts wrung their hands with worry.

"It became clear that if we wanted to have a bigger impact on Olympic hockey, then we'd need to develop more pros," recalled Bob Mancini, the head coach at Michigan Tech, who was attending the World Hockey Summit in Boston in the summer of '96. "The national office saw that we were struggling as a nation at the World Junior Championships and were looking for a way to bring together our top players at the age somewhere around sixteen, seventeen . . . so we could compete on the world stage."

The International Ice Hockey Federation (IIHF) governs hockey at the international level and hosts a series of age-specific annual tournaments that bring the best young players into fierce competition with one another. The U18s are for players eighteen and under, and the U20 World Junior Champions are open to twenty-year-olds and below. Since the tournaments' inception in 1977, both the World Juniors and the U18s had been dominated by Canada and the Soviet Union. Team USA had come to expect little, and usually got it. "We had been embarrassed for two, three years in a row," said Jeff Jackson, head coach of the '95 team. "There was such a lack of pride for American players to play in that tournament."

The Canadians had professionalized their amateur development system; Sweden and Finland had followed suit, determined to capture talent early and cultivate it in a sustained and rigorous fashion. Even after the fall of the Soviet Union, the Russians remained competitive at the IIHF tournaments, medaling at the World Juniors every year but one in the 1990s. Those countries were blessed with the long winters that brought restless children out onto frozen ponds and lakes, day after day, year after year. The entire US approach to the game of hockey, in contrast, was decentralized and unfocused on international competition. If Team USA couldn't start winning, the young talent would just play baseball or basketball or football instead.

Even Blake Geoffrion, the scion of one of the great North American hockey families, spent his spring weekends in the mid-1990s fielding grounders and taking batting practice in the Williamson County Youth Baseball league. He was good, too, a natural athlete as comfortable swinging a baseball bat as he was wielding a hockey stick. And the ball fields were a whole lot shorter drive than the Centennial Sportsplex ice rink in Nashville. For Blake and other kids of his generation, the Miracle on Ice was ancient history. Without new heroes with new medals draped around their necks, those young athletes might be lost to hockey forever. Little did he know that changes were being contemplated that might alter not only his future and the futures of his fellow Pee Wee hockey wunderkinds but also the entire future of the sport south of the forty-ninth parallel.

The executive committee of USA Hockey's board of directors tasked Ron DeGregorio, chair of the organization's International Council, with forging the path these young men would travel, and he knew all about the dearth of US-born talent in professional hockey. In that dire spring of '96, DeGregorio had a moment of militaristic inspiration. ROTC programs on college campuses provided reserve officers for the US military, but the elite officer corps (the regular army) came from the US Military Academy at West Point, which demanded the highest standards from its applicants and then provided them with the finest training the country had to offer. The National Team Development Program (NTDP), as it would come to be called, was going to be West Point for hockey—a *de-paht-ment*, in DeGregorio's New England elocution, focused strictly on development.

DeGregorio and USA Hockey executive director Dave Ogrean had a vision: forty-eight of the country's best young players, housed near a world-class practice facility, facing the toughest competition over the course of the full school year. Eight unforgiving months away from family, with strength, conditioning, nutritional discipline, and top-tier coaches to mold raw talent into explosive ability from blue line to blue line. Two teams, one for kids under age seventeen and one for those under eighteen. Skills development would be hammered into the thick skulls of these chosen teenagers, setting them on a path not just to international medals and Division I scholarships but also to hockey's biggest stages: the NHL and the Olympics. The new program would replace the existing haphazard system, which threatened to allow un-polished promise, like that of Blake Geoffrion in Tennessee and Patrick Kane in New York, to slip away.

The program would need to be conveniently located so that games could be played against teams in the major junior leagues and versus col-lege teams, though international competitions would of course be the true marker of the NTDP's success. From their home arena, the boys would venture into the world, wearing USA jerseys and armed with sticks freshly taped for battle against the Swedes, the Finns, the Czechs, Slovaks, Russians. And the Canadians. These new Team USA squads would replicate the Long Gray Line of West Point with the Long Red, White, and Blue Line of the NTDP, molding an elite unit of on-ice warriors wearing sharpened skates rather than polished boots.

All they needed was a leader.

~

College hockey programs guard their head coaches as misers guard their gold, so the search for an NTDP head coach was conducted in secret. Michigan native Jeff Jackson had quickly become a coaching sensation at tiny Lake Superior State University, where he'd taken over as head coach in 1990 and promptly led the program to six consecutive NCAA tournament appearances, three trips to the finals, and two national championships. In the spring of 1996, he was hustled quietly to USA Hockey's Colorado Springs headquarters, where he was first discreetly consulted about the state of US hockey and then indoctrinated into the grand conspiracy to launch a national development program.

Jackson had impressed the USA Hockey executives with his track record, but his vision for developing hockey confirmed that he was the man to pioneer this new initiative. DeGregorio and Ogrean hired him, convinced that he could envision and execute the concept of an all-encompassing, long-term program needed to put Team USA on an even footing with the best that Canada and Europe had to offer. Each year, USA Hockey would craft a roster for the World Junior Championships from among current NTDP players as well as program alumni playing for collegiate or major junior programs who were still under twenty years old and tournament eligible. The three men shook hands and parted ways temporarily, with DeGregorio and Ogrean determined to find funding and take on hockey's entrenched interests.

Jackson's hiring was announced at the World Hockey Summit in July 1996 in Boston. Bob Mancini, who had been an assistant with Jackson at Lake Superior State, was still digesting his wedding cake when he got the call to come to Massachusetts to interview for the NTDP's assistant coach position. "Right before our honeymoon, I convinced my wife it would be a good idea to go to Boston. And after they offered me the job, I had to go back to my hotel room and tell my wife of three days, 'Hey, we're moving!'" She started a packing list on the hotel stationery.

Hockey insiders refer to the geographic pillars of the US game as the Three *M*s—Massachusetts, Michigan, and Minnesota. And as DeGregorio and Ogrean knew better than most, for the diehards, regionalism is tribalism. In addition to convincing the board of USA Hockey to spend a significant chunk of its budget on two teams totaling just forty-eight players, the executives would have to choose one of the Three *M*s to serve as the headquarters for their shiny new program, a decision to which the others were sure to object. They chose Ann Arbor, Michigan.

Coaches and parents from Massachusetts and Minnesota had plenty to say about that.

~

The location of the new national program was announced at an international exhibition tournament in Lacombe, Alberta, causing parents and kids alike to gape in disbelief. *Michigan?* Hand Red Berenson a stocked pond of hockey talent for the University of Michigan program? Voluntarily take the legs out from the good Minnesota and Massachusetts schools that had waited patiently for years for this crop of kids to blossom into the superstar recruits everyone had been projecting since Pee Wees? Patriotic fervor and eight months of first-class competition, coaching, training, and exposure were enticing draws, but this amounted to sheer treason.

Future Hobey Baker winner Jordan Leopold was the first Minnesotan to announce his commitment to the fledgling NTDP. Seven more from his home state would follow, accounting for one-sixth of the NTDP players. The fury of a slighted Minnesota hockey community quickly descended on their teenage heads. "I knew it was going to be tough for people to understand here in Minnesota, but I didn't realize it was going to cause such a ruckus," said Leopold. "I remember being on a radio talk show with [former NHL player] Dave Snuggerud, him being an icon in Minnesota as far as hockey goes, and him just reaming my ass about how I could leave Minnesota hockey and the talent pool is just as good here as anywhere else. But truth be known, it isn't. It isn't." Nine hundred miles to the south, at the Centennial Sportsplex in Nashville, Blake Geoffrion was learning the same lesson. Anyone who wanted to play with the best needed to leave home.

The old school puckheads, the self-anointed keepers of the game, felt betrayed by the departure of this cadre of ascendant stars just when they were getting good. "They were afraid that the kids from Minnesota who went to play in Ann Arbor wouldn't go back to play at the U [of Minnesota], at St. Cloud [State University]. Same with the Boston schools. Everyone thought, 'Oh my god, these players are all going to

go to Michigan, and then play for Michigan and Michigan State,'"
remembered Mancini. Some people saw it as a cruel trick to play on the
other two *Ms*, the same crucibles that had brought Mike Eruzione, Rob
McClanahan, and most of the other 1980 Miracle team members into
the world.

"They worked the shit out of us that first year," said Leopold. "They
wanted to see if we were going to survive." The hopes of the entire US
hockey community rested on the sore, bruised, but slowly broadening
shoulders of four dozen teenagers, pulled away from home and nearly
as terrified as the coaches tasked with their development.

~

Games and practices and team meetings from that first winter of 1998
tended to blur together: *Who could distinguish dates when weeks turned
into months and games merely punctuated an endless rotation of practices,
lifting sessions, tape sessions, team runs, more practices, scrimmages, history
class, algebra class, homework, still more practices, and finally a bus ride
to some godforsaken town on the Michigan–Ontario border.* And while
the goons of the Ontario Hockey League flattened Team USA in one
bruising game after another, the coaches dashed back and forth from
Michigan to Colorado Springs, tightening their laces for one boardroom battle after another.

Those early teams were not focused on amassing wins during the
regular season, and their record reflected it. They didn't cross the .500
mark in the first two seasons, and the long-term vision hadn't begun to
take hold in time for the 1999 IIHF World Juniors, when the team yet
again failed to make the medal podium. Jackson and Mancini preached
the gospel of skills fundamentals ad nauseum, layering toughness and
character growth on top of skating and puck handling and passing and
shooting, refusing to be distracted by a lopsided win-loss record.

Frustration with the program long predated the first drop of the
puck, with unwavering opposition on predictable territorial grounds.
The volunteer board of USA Hockey directors was vigilant and vocal in
its opposition to the NTDP. "They verbally attacked Jeff [Jackson] and
I for how we were running the program," Mancini recalled.

One board meeting turned so sour that Jackson stormed out and drove to the airport. The nascent NTDP program was teetering on the edge, its fate uncertain and with it the future of USA Hockey.

~

By the fall of 1999, after two seasons of NTDP experimentation, the foundation that Jackson, Mancini, and Ogrean had so painstakingly laid in Ann Arbor was starting to crumble under the weight of organizational politics. Ogrean departed as executive director that summer, hired away by the US Olympic Committee, and his leaving exposed Jackson and Mancini to a knife in the back from the volunteer board back in Colorado Springs. Their team had limped to a 17–37 record in the North American Hockey League that second season, and the Team USA World Juniors squad once again missed the medal round. But Jackson hadn't lost faith just yet. His World Juniors team for the upcoming winter 2000 tournament was stacked with the kids they had recruited for that first NTDP year, players who had moved on to the college ranks but still carried the memory of the red, white, and blue team chemistry. Would the competition in Sweden, the host nation, be stiff? Absolutely. The Swedes were rumored to be lightning on ice, led by identical twins Daniel and Henrik Sedin, who dazzled with their effortless cycling and one-two passing that so often set up a sneaky shot past the goalie.

The January 2000 tournament was a formidable test, the culmination of everything the team had worked toward. Goalie Rick DiPietro, in the quarterfinals against Sweden, blocked one clever wrister after another, slapping away each Sedin shot even as the Swedes were being handed man-advantage scoring opportunities left and right. "We were up against some pretty good Russian refereeing," remembered Jackson. Yet he watched as their team came to life with a fire born of years of shared adversity. Playing shorthanded for the last four minutes of the game, Team USA closed it out with authority, defeating the Swedes 5–1.

The US players stood at the edge of medal contention, still sizzling after their takedown of the hometown favorites. Much hung in the balance as the hockey world watched; the NTDP finally had its chance to prove the promise of its vision. But that New Year's Eve, days before the semifinal against the burly Czechs, Jackson's mother suffered a stroke, and he rushed home to Michigan. Without its fiery coach, Team USA lost 4–1 and then endured a heartbreaking shootout defeat against Team Canada in the bronze medal game. To the NTDP's believers, it was a near miss. To its naysayers, it proved what they knew all along: too much money and energy had been spent on too few players for too little in return. The clamor for change reached a crescendo, and Jackson and Mancini were fired the following summer. No one—the USA Hockey volunteer board, the organization's executives, or the coaching candidates they had lined up for interviews—knew how much longer the experiment would last.

A month after the US squad slouched home, Blake Geoffrion turned twelve. Gone from his room were the toy race cars and the cowboy boots and spurs from an earlier stage of adolescence. His preteen walls screamed hockey. Posters, crossed sticks, trading cards, and trophies covered every inch. He was good, and Danny was proud. But no one outside of Blake's tiny Tennessee hockey community cared. His name wasn't yet on the lips of the prep school scouts or the junior league coaches. It certainly wasn't in the mix of those being considered for the fledgling—yet endangered—NTDP. Despite his bloodlines, Blake was simply a skinny Pee Wee hockey player from Brentwood. As a concept, though, Blake fit exactly the profile that Colorado Springs and Ann Arbor were fighting and feuding over.

His parents, rushing from tournament to tournament, had no time to consider where hockey in America was headed or how or why. They could barely manage to keep schedules straight and skates sharpened and their sons from brawling in the back seat. They left the future of USA Hockey to others, not knowing that their precocious son would soon be asked to don the colors of his country on the international stage.

∾

"Shoot more, shoot from anywhere, pucks go off asses and go in the net! More shots on the net!" Mike Eaves was fired up. He scrawled inch-high words across the whiteboard in black marker. Nearly two dozen players stared grimly ahead, unblinking in the face of profane exhortation, desperately avoiding eye contact with the finger-wagging figure in front of them, shaggy hair dripping sweat into their eyes.

USA Hockey had hired Eaves to replace Jeff Jackson in 2000, and here his team was, in the gold medal game of the 2002 IIHF U18 World Championships in Piešťany, Slovakia. "The jockey knew the horses and the horses knew the jockey," thought USA Hockey executive Ron DeGregorio, staring at the whiteboard.

Eaves had been a superstar forward at the University of Wisconsin before embarking on a seven-year NHL playing career. He was the Badgers' all-time leading points scorer and had won a national championship in 1977. He was never smooth—his coach once compared his churning legs to an eggbeater on the ice—but his obsessive self-motivation drove him far beyond the point where natural talent petered out. "Mike gets as much out of himself as any player I've ever coached," declared the legendary Bob Johnson. Eaves's intensity delighted his coach. It left others, teammates and opponents alike, absolutely petrified.

Injuries cut short Eaves's NHL career, and he'd been honing his craft off the ice as an assistant coach, most recently with the Pittsburgh Penguins under Herb Brooks, when USA Hockey invited him to interview for the NTDP gig in 2002. Moe Mantha, a former Penguin player himself, would be the coach of the U17 team. While both Mantha and Eaves were fresh faces inside the world of USA Hockey, they faced the same challenges as their predecessors. An increasingly vocal contingent was baying for the blood of the dollar-sucking, talent-squandering program. Those still defending the NTDP knew that something had to change. The Mike 'n' Moe Era needed to become the Win Now Era.

And fast.

~

Program recruiting shifted from a focus on players who could be developed into viable NHL prospects down the line to a focus on stockpiling more polished players who could score. A *lot*, and in a hurry—first in the U17 Challenge, then at the U18 IIHF World Championships, and finally at the U20 World Juniors, where success had proven so elusive.

"You can't teach six foot five" had been an oft-repeated saying under Jackson, frequently grumbled at screens flickering with prep-school game tape. But Eaves was looking for something different, and his search took him beyond the Three Ms. Brett Sterling, for example, was the right kind of different.

Even wearing skates, he'd never top five-foot-seven. But the diminutive Jewish kid out of Los Angeles had unbelievable touch, on-ice speed that turned necks into rubber, and a fiery competitive drive. Most important, he lived to score goals. As a skinny sixteen-year-old in his first year with the NTDP, Sterling put up a dazzling twenty-nine goals in the North American Hockey League, against the same class of older players who had pushed around Jackson's team just a few years earlier. Sterling eventually suited up with three NHL teams over an eighteen-year professional career.

"We were focused on getting the right kids that fit the program, with the right character, right attitude," said Eaves. "We looked for the building blocks of a team to provide balance: skill guys, the foot soldiers, guys that would get in the corners and do the dirty work, that would learn to wear the red, white, and blue with pride. They all came in with skinny little runt necks, anyway." Eaves, Mantha, and Ken Martel saw individual players as puzzle pieces in a larger system, one newly designed to secure medals.

But medals would be tough. The U18s featured a star-studded pool of opponents, including one kid who played on the first line for Team Russia with the name Ovechkin stretched across his shoulders, a name that would one day catch the glint of the Stanley Cup as he lifted it high into the air.

~

The doors of the Easton Arena in Piešt'any swung inward as Team USA strolled into the aging Slovak facility for the 2002 U18 IIHF World Championships. Eaves's squad may not have known it, but the nondescript arena had borne witness to yet another mighty Cold War hockey clash, the "Punch-Up in Piešťany," that was as memorable for Canadians as the Miracle on Ice was for their counterparts south of the border. That bench-clearing brawl between the Canadian and Soviet U20 teams, had cemented the World Juniors tournament in the national consciousness of the Canadian public and had, by extension, made it an enduring fixture in the world of international hockey competition.

Eaves and his young assistant, John Hynes, had assembled a squad brimming with confidence and team chemistry in preparation for the tournament, and it showed in the early rounds. The US team steamrolled one opponent after another—first Belarus (9–0), then Ukraine (10–0), Finland (3–2), and Sweden (6–2)—before moving on to the elimination round and smashing Team Canada 10–3 in a deliciously satisfying game that saw Eaves's squad pot three unanswered goals in the final period alone. On April 21, 2002, after two weeks of light-'em-up hockey, Zach Parise found himself staring across the face-off circle at a fresh-faced young Russian, Alexander Ovechkin. Ovechkin later dubbed the Great Eight while wearing No. 8 as captain of the Washington Capitals, had already tickled the twine thirteen times in seven games. He was unstoppable. He skated with genius in his toes. And his sinewy frame stood between Team USA and the medals and affirmation they so desperately wanted.

$\sim$

Brrraaaaannnngg. Brrraaaaannnngg. David Booth's heart raced inside his Team USA sweater as he pumped his fist, gliding into the suffocating embrace of his linemates. He had just smashed through Russian defenders to bury his second goal of the period, making the score 2–0. But back on the bench, his teammates gnawed at their mouthguards, eyes flickering to the clock as the seconds ticked by. Because of the tournament's tiebreaker rules, a failure to beat the previously undefeated Russians by two or more goals would mean that Team USA would slink home with a silver medal and another near miss. The second period crept by without another tally. As the third period began, US players leaned over the boards, staring as teammates dropped to their knees and blocked one shot after another, eating seconds off the clock, willing the passage of time to accelerate. Then *Brrraaaaannnngg*. It was a dagger to the watching skaters, a smashing Ovechkin slap shot into the back of the US net. Though the United States was still ahead by one goal, they were in danger of losing the whole thing.

"Jimmy!" Coach Eaves gestured wildly at his goaltender, who lowered his head and dug desperately for the bench. An extra skater went over the boards, six white jerseys now circling around the ice, Team USA's unattended net watching as distant players flung passes around the Russian zone. Slap, settle, drag, the *swish, fwap, swish, fwap* of crisp passes mesmerized onlookers and participants alike.

The puck bounced off the pads of the Russian goaltender, and a US player captured the rebound and fed it to Parise up top. Windup, shot, SCORE! The clock ticked down: five, four, three, two . . . and it was all over. Pandemonium. The US teens embraced in gratified exhaustion. It had been the longest third period of their short lives.

Eaves's team wore its ice packs as badges of honor, swaggering their way down the tunnel. "Some of 'em played the game with a lot of pain," said Mantha. "But I'm pretty sure if they could do it, they'd do it all over again."

～

For all of the Stanley Cups, the scoring titles, all-star selections, and hall-of-fame inductions, no member of the famed Geoffrion-Morenz family had ever suited up for their country in international play, stood for the national anthem with the flag on his sleeve matching the one fluttering above his head. A bit wistfully, Danny had always told his boys what an unbelievable honor it was to play for national pride. So had Bernie.

The NTDP program that Blake Geoffrion joined in the fall of 2004 bore little resemblance to the upstart squads of the late 1990s. Program critics had gone quiet for the moment, shushed by the sparkling hardware now dazzling visitors to Colorado Springs. The 2002 U18 trophy, a gleaming plate engraved with the IIHF logo, stood on the shelf next to the most coveted symbol of success, the 2004 IIHF World Junior Championship trophy. John Hynes had taken over as head coach when Mike Eaves moved on to the University of Wisconsin. Hynes was in charge of the 1988 birth year team (the '88s, in NTDP-speak); he shepherded the players through their U17 season in the North American Hockey League, preparation for their eventual pursuit of another IIHF gold medal at the U18s. Long gone were the days of cajoling Minnesota and Massachusetts families into loaning their sons to Michigan. "The massive success, even over international teams . . . really started to turn with the ability to get great players to come," said Hynes. He and the rest of the NTDP staff had been watching Boom Boom Geoffrion's grandson develop at Culver Military Academy, slowly transforming his raw hockey skill and athleticism into scoring dynamism. Blake had gotten his size early, a crucial complement to the smaller, slighter players with whom he'd share a line. It was time to bring him into the USA Hockey fold.

"After my sophomore year, I went to the USA Hockey festival up at St. Cloud State," Blake remembered. "I had a really good tournament, playing really well, and NTDP, Ken Martel and David Quinn [the U17 coach] were kind of sniffing around. They pulled me into a locker room and said, 'We love the way you play; we want to offer you a spot on the National Development Program for next year." They had been watching him for two years at Culver and hearing about him for even longer—ever since he had started playing in those Southeastern District USA Hockey tournaments as a twelve-year-old. Technically, he still had to go through tryouts, but the coaches knew the *right kind of player* when they saw one.

Blake knew plenty about the program by then. He knew that Eaves had coached the U18 team to USA Hockey's first-ever gold medal in 2002 and had come back to lead the U20 squad to a gold medal, another first, at the 2004 World Junior Championships. He knew that the focus on skills development was as obsessive as the fixation on strength and conditioning and that if he ever wanted to reach the NHL, he would need to add muscle mass to his lean frame, just as he would need to continue to add to the foundation of skating, passing, and shooting fundamentals he had been honing at Culver. Stan Butler, an old friend of Danny's, had been making the hard sell to Blake to come play in the Ontario Hockey League, and the baseball boosters back in Middle Tennessee hadn't stopped calling either. But the professionalism of the NTDP staff—from the coaches who never let a bad habit slip without correction to the trainers who brought an unrivaled depth of nutrition and weightlifting expertise to their young charges—made Blake's choice a no-brainer. He once again called his dad to again ask about quitting a hockey program. This time, Danny responded with a boisterous endorsement.

Blake's dream of playing in the NHL suddenly seemed one step closer.

The dazzling white sweaters stamped with *USA* reminded Blake and his new teammates that they had at last reached the big time. Always the stars back home, they felt as though they had been anointed after arriving in Ann Arbor—the young princes of the rink, crowned as national standard-bearers for the game; spotless pads and blockers; new sticks, coaches, and trainers, nudging the players along to an even higher plane of achievement. NHL scouts were a regular presence at their games, covetously eyeing the next generation of highlight makers and league leaders. Each player was assigned a billet family to live with, and teachers at one of three local high schools catered to the demands of their unrelenting schedule of practices and games, tournaments, and travel. A small army of trainers and equipment managers indulged their every on-ice whim.

The gear was so pristine, so high-end, that it made some of the new arrivals nervous just to pick it up. *How much is all this stuff going to cost?* thought Blake. *I might need to call my parents.* When the trainers assured him that, no, everything had already been paid for, the full weight of his country's investment in his future began to dawn on him.

Blake's linemate was Patrick Kane, a young phenom whose slight build belied the stunning hockey instinct hidden within his silky mitts. Growing up in Buffalo, New York, he had clashed frequently with elite competition from across the nearby Canadian border. One player in particular always seemed to be across the face-off circle: Jonathan Toews. These clashes were early skirmishes in the much bigger, nastier border battle in which Blake Geoffrion would soon play a critical part.

The glistening new equipment was sweat-soaked after the first practice. "I want you two inches past the line!" Hynes barked as the players raced from end line to red line to blue line. His regimen was steeped in a drive for constant refinement and a focus on core skills, ever more challenging and complex and demanding on the evolving squad toiling under his watch. Nearly every player arrived as a hotshot scorer, yet each had to be hammered into a new shape to fit within the NTDP system, to play for team over self, country above all.

Blake was a natural fit. His time at Culver had instilled discipline and coachability that others lacked.

"He had such an infectious personality," recalled Hynes. "He played a vital role for two years on the team, and quickly became one of the leaders. It was Blake who played the role as the 'glue guy,' who could relate to the coaches and to the players who weren't the best on the team while also hanging with Kane and Erik Johnson, guys who were more high-profile. He had all the things you can't teach as a coach."

But the big kid from Tennessee started slowly, just as he had at Culver. His coaches watched him miss the net, then overcorrect, then miss again, consumed by the need for points. They watched him struggle to find a clear role for himself; to put his size to use in the corners, in front of the net, in the face-off circles; to stay hungry without letting his competitiveness blind him to the subtle shifts always happening within the game. Hynes warned him that the goals wouldn't come until he could marry his self-worth with a role on the team. Blake heard it all. He thought he understood. He just could not make his body respond. The NTDP schedule was a step up in class, and as one game after another slipped by without a goal, his frustration began to build.

"By Christmas, I had fewer points than the two goalies; one goal and one assist, and each of them had three assists." He was embarrassed, maybe even depressed. His usual jovial, optimistic outlook was clouded by the barren stat sheet beneath his last name.

Hynes had seen this before. "Most of the time when you get to that level, there's a reason why. They were point producers coming in and were so consumed by points as the end result. I think that was a little bit of Blake."

While casual observers measure achievement only by wins and losses, sporting insiders know that good coaching recognizes more than just absolute outcomes, instead honing natural ability over time. Most players join elite teams with hot hands, but they can't all score every goal, every game. Not if they want to play on a winning team. But Blake was a Geoffrion, the grandson of the inventor of the slap shot and the great-grandson of hockey's original scoring superstar. Anyone telling him to subjugate his need for goals better have a damn good reason why.

Hynes sent Blake home to clear his head over the Christmas holidays. "We'll meet you in Alberta," he said, reassuring Blake that he'd have a top line spot for the New Year's tournament. Before Blake stepped back on the ice for the next game, his coach wanted to try a whole new approach.

~

"I want you to be the best defensive forward you can be," Hynes insisted, gripping the young man's shoulder. Blake's deep blue eyes gazed back in disbelief. "Win every single faceoff, get down on your knees to block shots. You, Ryan Flynn, Rhett Rakhshani—you guys are going to be my shutdown line."

This was a revolutionary reversal for Blake, a kid who had been weaving through opponents and burying goals since his Pee Wee years. Thinking back to all of those hours in his backyard in Brentwood, imitating his Pappy, he had been practicing shot *making*, not shot *blocking*. Every team he had ever played for, up to and including Team USA, had wanted him precisely because he could score goals. But Culver had taught him more than just marching and shoe polishing. He knew how to take an order, and he trusted his coach. Even a born leader knows when to follow.

I'm gonna need new shin pads, he thought. Under Hynes's tutelage, Blake began to envision himself as a baseball catcher behind the plate, a spring-loaded shot blocking machine, an enthusiastic collector of cuts and bruises and the occasional broken rib. Some hotshot players might have found such a role beneath them. Blake internalized the counsel, then began to pass the message along to his recalcitrant body. He ran drill after sweaty drill, dropping to the ice, leaping back up again, steeling his determination not to flinch in the face of a screaming wrist shot rifling toward him from mere feet away. He obsessively reviewed tape with Coach Hynes, marching onto the staff floor unannounced with a confidence that belied his young age, willing to share about his own life and to listen, unabashedly baring his thoughts and feelings and the gaps in his knowledge. "In all my years in the program, I never had someone like him," remembered Hynes. "He really had an old soul, a contagious personality."

Blake's willingness to transform his role on the ice for the betterment of his team was a product of the trust he shared with his coach and the humility so rarely possessed by someone with such a storied pedigree. It confirmed what the coaches who had first spotted him had sensed: here was the right kind of player—coachable, talented, and selfless. And it reaffirmed the original vision that had been laid out nearly a decade earlier: with elite coaching and mentoring offered for months on end without interruption, elite US players could be developed to form the basis for winning teams.

The U17 squad was up against serious competition in the World Challenge tournament in Lethbridge, Alberta. Hockey Canada was represented by three regional teams, every one of which was an offensive powerhouse. Jonathan Toews, Ryan White, and Jordan Staal made up Canada West's top line, each a future NHL player lacing up in front of a friendly home crowd. The US players won two of their four games in the preliminary round but failed to advance to the semifinals, finishing fourth overall. It was the first real adversity the team had faced. But Hynes could see the team coalescing around a core, and Blake, now playing as a two-way forward, knew that he was a part of it.

Ignoring his rapidly multiplying bruises, Blake had thrived on the penalty kill and had still managed to score five points in three games as his body relaxed and the puck began to bounce his way. The cliché of the "two-hundred-foot player" is one of the most overused in hockey: of course every coach wants players who can skate end-to-end, equally comfortable scoring goals and stopping them. Yet doing so requires a willingness to learn and a natural talent, paired with size, that few really possess. The Lethbridge tournament was a pivotal moment for a young man still finding his path, an identity all his own, one that would bring him goals and glory in the years to come.

"Even from the first year, leading into the second year, it was all about winning a medal" at the U18 World Championships, reflected Blake. This group of players, like all young hockey elites, perpetually carried the weight of their birth year with them. Individual games were quickly forgotten, but the years stood distinct. Coach Hynes relentlessly drove them toward the 2006 U18 World Championships. An all-star US team led by Wisconsin native Phil Kessel, snagged a second gold medal for the NTDP at the April 2005 U18s in the Czech Republic. The possibility of going back-to-back at a time when Canada was producing generational greats on a yearly basis? A second gold medal could cement the program, silence the skeptics, and redefine US competitiveness on the international stage.

It seemed bold, hubristic even, to dream that big, yet it also seemed fitting for a program suddenly imbued with overwhelming confidence. Blake Geoffrion had fully embraced his new two-way approach, perfectly cementing the vital power-play unit on the hardnosed, grind-it-out squad that Hynes had built.

The coaches were driving their team to a gold medal, and they never let their players forget it. The coaches craved the respect that repeat championships offered, the kind of career-defining success that could keep them employed and keep them climbing or prevent them from slipping down the coaching ladder, the haunting fear that follows every coach through every season. The bigwigs at USA Hockey wanted recognition and respect at home and abroad for the garden of budding hockey stars they had sowed through their still-young development program. The players themselves, well . . . they wanted all those things. But they were also teenagers, and the sight of scouts wearing pullovers featuring the logos of NHL teams set them to whispering and giggling. Sustained concentration at that age is a fool's errand. Offer distraction and temptation in the form of NHL scout attention, and focus soon becomes vaporous. During that 2005–6 season, scouts were a regular presence in the bleachers at NTDP games. A few regional amateur scouts usually showed up whenever Team USA came to their area, generally causing minimal disruption thanks to the barking and threats of punishment from Coach Hynes.

The U18 Championships would be a different matter entirely. The IIHF had chosen Ängelholm and Halmstad, two towns in southern Sweden, to host the 2006 U18s. The arenas would be filled with fans— and with scouts from every NHL team holding clipboards and video cameras aimed at the players on the ice. The 2004–5 NHL season had been lost due to a lockout, and front offices were more desperate than ever to secure the rights of young and talented players, especially with the new salary cap in place. The puck was set to drop in Sweden on April 12, 2006, with Team USA first facing off against the Russians. On June 24, the NHL draft would take place. As the team marched through that season, busing and flying from game to game, the players did not necessarily know when, where, or against whom they would be playing next. But those two dates lingered in their consciousness.

When the NHL released its midseason prospect rankings in January, the players' hooting could be heard from a mile away. A record twelve US-born players were ranked in the first round. The NTDP's own Erik Johnson, already a formidable blueliner as a teenager, was ranked at No. 1 in the world! Phil Kessel, an NTDP graduate, was No. 2. Canadian superstar Jonathan Toews was No. 3, fresh off yet another World Junior Championships gold medal. Blake was No. 45, just outside the first round, with one more thing to prove in Sweden.

Blake also knew firsthand the dangers of fixating on draft order. He had grown up in the home of an NHL first-round draft pick: Danny had been taken eighth overall in 1978, only to find himself out of the league three years later, having never scored a goal for the Montreal Canadiens, the team that had drafted him.

The malady of distracted overconfidence was on full display a few weeks after the NHL predraft rankings were released. Team USA was playing in an international exhibition tournament—and playing poorly. Watching errant shots follow sloppy passes, Coach Hynes was stoic, silently fuming at the lack of hustle. *Losing happened. Losing in that fashion was unacceptable.* In their first practice back at the Cube, their home rink, sweat dripped off their noses as coaches drove players through drill after drill.

"If you're not going to work in the tournament, we're gonna work you now!" Hynes shouted, demanding that they hurl their bodies from one end of the ice to the other, blue line back, red line back. "Don't you ever give up on the puck!" reverberated through the rink as muscles groaned in agony.

"Past the line! Your mental toughness comes from in here!"

After nearly two years of intense practices, of "that Hynesy shit, running us into the ground," the team was used to aching exhaustion. But this was worse. But it was also the jolt they needed. In their ears rang their coach's mantra—a dictum as well as a warning: Champions walk together forever.

The clock was ticking.

~

Hynes's intrepid young skaters soon returned to form, but then tragedy struck in February, two months before the long-awaited trip to Sweden. At an exhibition game against the Rochester Institute of Technology, NTDP defenseman Trent Palm collided with an opposing player and went cartwheeling through the air. His skate slashed teammate Chris Atkinson's neck from ear to collarbone, clipping his jugular vein. Blood spurted on the ice. Players and fans turned away.

The scene unfolded in slow motion for Atkinson. He had been looking at the play, and when Palm got flipped, he saw the skate swinging toward him. He closed his eyes, then felt himself falling. Was his collarbone broken? His left arm was numb, dangling uselessly. He felt blood flow down his neck, down onto the ice.

Medics raced Atkinson off on a stretcher, his blood staining the white jersey of Team USA trainer Dave Cotner. Entering the tunnel, Atkinson turned his eyes toward his team's bench. The ashen faces of his teammates met his gaze. All stood silenced with fear. Fear for their teammate. Fear, suddenly, of a game they had always played without consequence.

Atkinson's absence weighed heavily on Blake Geoffrion and his team- mates. Atkinson was well-liked, his jokes a welcome distraction from the seriousness of their training just as his forechecking was dependable in the grittiest of games. For Team USA, the upcoming tournament now meant even more.

On March 10, only a few weeks after Atkinson's injury, Blake stepped off the ice after a road game to find his coach waiting with a message. The piece of paper thrust into his hand bore two simple, chilling words. *Call Nana.*

Boom Boom Geoffrion had never seemed destined for old age, but he reached it anyway. His nose had been broken nine times and his skin had been repaired with more than four hundred stitches over a sixteen-year run in the National Hockey League. The most terrifying moment of his career, though, came during a routine practice in 1958, when he collapsed after suffering a ruptured bowel and was rushed to a Montreal hospital, where a priest read the last rites. Within weeks, however, Boom Boom was back on the ice, and a little more than a month later he scored the winning goal to secure the Habs' third Stanley Cup in three years.

The twinkle in Bernie Geoffrion's eye had always been irrepressible. Through all the stops and starts, concussions and injuries, the affronts of coaching stints cut short and a career spent in the shadow of other Canadien legends, despite a fifty-goal season in 1960–61 and an MVP award to top it off, and through the ultimate indignity of being passed over for the honor of wearing the captain's *C*—through it all, the gleam and the grin never faded.

He was nineteen, fresh off his rookie season with Montreal, when he met Marlene Morenz and used his wit and guile to talk her into a date.

Wedged romantically in the crowded seats of the Montreal Forum, two boxers slugging it out in the ring below, he nudged her and pointed up toward the rafters: "You see your father's number, hanging up there? One day, mine will be hanging right next to it."

The two married not long after, and Bernie spent the next two decades shooting and scoring in front of a packed house at the Forum, each season building his growing legend. Bernie had lived long enough to see one of his grandsons, Blake, play for Team USA, a fiercely proud grandfather even if his loyalty to Canada led him to make a point of walking across the logo on the locker room floor whenever he came to visit Ann Arbor. And now that grandson stood with the phone pressed to his ear, in a hockey rink, the faint, familiar sounds of clattering sticks echoing through to the other end of the line.

"Your Pappy hasn't spoken for a few days, but the doctors assure me he can hear through the phone when I hold it up to his ear." She did, and Blake spoke, thickly, squeezing out the words: "I scored two slap shot goals tonight, Pappy. I love you, and I'll miss you always."

Silence for a few seconds, and then a faded, weak voice murmured, "It's about time."

Those were the last words Bernard Geoffrion spoke before his eyes closed forever. He died of stomach cancer in the early morning hours of March 11, 2006.

That date had already been circled on the Geoffrions' calendar for months. Boom Boom's No. 5 was set to be retired by the Canadiens that day. All the members of the family were supposed to fly in, and Kelly had even planned to make a little vacation out of it. Danny would introduce his father and then stand back a respectful distance and cede the microphone to Boom Boom, who would quiet the elated crowd as they cheered on their living legend. The Canadiens were scheduled to play the Rangers, the only other NHL team for which Boom Boom had ever laced up, and every player would wear a bright, white No. 5 sweater during warmups.

But when Danny took his place in front of the microphone that night, it was not to introduce his father but to eulogize him.

"Dad," Danny said, "your family loves you more than you'll ever know."

Kelly stood off to the side, with Marlene and the boys, all holding each other, leaning inward for support, their faces wet with tears. A tribute video played across the screen, the old black-and-white images flickering as his signature slap shot boomed again and again to the soundtrack of Sinatra's "My Way." Richard Garneau, the master of ceremonies, asked the crowd for a moment of silence, and the arena fell still.

Nothing could be heard. Nothing, that is, but the sound of thousands weeping. The seconds crept by, the heart of a city aching with loss, and then all eyes turned upward, rapt, and sobs turned to cheers. The banner with "Morenz 7," descended slowly from the rafters, stopping halfway to the ice. Up rose the red banner with its white "Geoffrion 5." The two names, forever linked, met in the middle, then ascended together.

Blake had never really understood the magnitude of the legacy he had inherited until he was whisked to Quebec on March 11, a date that had already been made famous by his great grandfather's funeral. Only when customs agents sought out his family waiting in the passport line at the Montreal airport and when the comforting hands of dozens of strangers reached out to pat the Geoffrions' shoulders in sympathy, whispering condolences in English and in French, did he begin to consider how much his grandfather had meant to so many for so long. *Wow*, thought Blake, *Pappy was a superstar.* His brain took him one step further. *And I'm a Geoffrion.*

Kelly, shepherding her boys onto Canadian soil, was struck by the same realization. For all the dinner checks that had been picked up by strangers over the years, the special invitations to league events and the carte blanche her sons had enjoyed in NHL locker rooms since their elementary school days, not until she saw her family standing arm in arm, resting against each other as the sorrow of so many descended upon then, did she truly understand that Boom Boom had been larger than life. And that now, with his passing, her sons would carry the weight of his legacy.

~

In April, the NTDP team departed for Sweden for the U18 World Championships. "Everyone was anxious, ready . . . everyone wanted a repeat," remembered Blake. One seat on the plane was empty. Chris Atkinson was left at home, the wound on his neck still healing.

In less than a decade, the NTDP had gone from a punching bag to a symbol of pride for the US hockey community. The team was on the cusp, ready to make medal contention an annual proposition. The possibility of winning three gold medals in five years was tantalizing and poetic—as well as a source of endless anxiety for the twenty-two young men who had grown under the leadership of Coach Hynes. Descending slowly through clouds over the Baltic Sea, the players dreamed about the medal ceremony. The thud of wheels on frozen asphalt shook them back to reality. *Sweden, boys. Time to suit up.*

Walking five-wide on the sidewalks of Halmstad or through the hallways of Ängelholm's Ishall Arena, their mere presence was imposing, a proclamation of physicality. The United States had arrived. Blake had filled out in the Cube's weight room, and so had Chris Summers. Erik Johnson had always been massive. Patrick Kane had taken to bumping his weight up on the official stat line by three, four pounds to look bigger on paper, a fact he would often exploit on the ice. He could easily disappear amid his larger teammates, only to resurface in the crease, poised and puck-hungry.

The chippy tone of the tournament was set early on: Team Russia jogged an extra lap just to crash through the Americans' flat-ground walkthrough, jostling shoulders and flashing dirty looks. Animosity wouldn't sustain the Russians, though, even if their team was stacked with future NHL players. They allowed two Bill Sweatt goals in the third period of their opening game against Blake and his teammates, with an empty netter in the closing seconds adding insult to injury. Final score: USA 4, Russia 2. Team USA steamrolled through the rest of the preliminary round, 9–0 over the Germans, 5–0 against the Czechs, and 12–1 to finish off lowly Belarus. The Czechs had lost their heads in that first encounter, but Hynes warned his players not to look past the squad in the semifinal rematch. Michael Frolík, a projected first rounder, was anchoring the top line for the Czech team, backed up by the ferocious Jakub Voráček and another goalscoring fiend, Jiří Tlustý, who would be drafted by the Toronto Maple Leafs in the first-round that summer.

In front of a sparse crowd, this time with elimination or advancement on the line, Team USA settled into a comfortable rhythm. Less than five minutes into the first period of the rematch against the Czechs, Blake crouched low in the neutral zone and muscled the puck back to defenseman Trent Palm, who sent it zipping across to Rhett Rakhshani, who chipped it into the corner. He chased it, wrenching a Czech player off the puck, before Blake scooped it up again, deked, and beat one defenseman, *vwoop*, then weaved past another, the puck glued to his stick. He finally burst past the net and flipped the puck back to Ryan Flynn, who slammed it stick-side past the goalie.

Jostling shoulders and elbows with their opponents, the American players grinned through their helmet cages. Up 3–1 heading into the third period, they were cruising, on their way to a second consecutive championship final for the program. "Everyone was so confident, happy," said Blake. Yet old-timer wisdom holds that a two-goal lead is the most dangerous in hockey. One penalty stacked up, then another, and with a five-on-three advantage, a Czech forward slipped one past Joe Palmer to close the gap. *Short memory, that's OK, let's play our game*, thought Blake. But with seven minutes left on the clock, the Czechs' knocked home another to tie the game. Smiles disappeared when the young US players realized how close they were to letting their moment slip away.

One American defenseman had been ejected in the second period for a game misconduct, and the team headed into the four-on-four overtime with aching muscles and an incomplete blue line. Fatigue pulled at muscles under both team sweaters, but if the US skaters panted with exhaustion, the Czechs panted louder, slower to skate up to the face-off circles for each puck drop. Players slipped and then scrambled back to their feet. The puck spun looping through the neutral zone, players swiping at it halfheartedly. At each break in the action, a bizarre soundtrack of '80s workout tracks pumped through the arena, mocking the dripping, cartoonish players clinging to the boards.

Fifty-five seconds into overtime, a kneeing penalty against Bill Sweatt left Team USA a man down. After killing the penalty, the US skaters got their own man advantage when a Czech forward was called for roughing. Kane was fresh off the ice but already shrieking in Hynes's ear, begging for another shift. "I'm ready. I'm ready!" Over the boards, and No. 27 raced through the offensive zone, snared the puck, flitted around defenders, and loosed a clean shot. The goalie turned it aside, but Luke Popko corralled the rebound and launched the puck back toward the net. Another shot and another rebound, this time to Kane's stick. He lunged forward and flicked the puck past the goalie, and the horn sounded. GOAL!

Twenty-one players piled recklessly onto their little forward as he dropped his stick and leapt into the air, only to be dragged back down by the crush of bodies. They had done it. Between them and the gold stood Finland—ironically, the same opponent that Team USA had faced after defeating the Soviets in the Miracle on Ice. Fate, once again, seemed on their side.

The 2006 tournament was televised in the United States, providing a timely burst of exposure and giving stateside fans the chance to follow every shift in real time. This team was poised for greatness, but so was the entire idea of a national development program. Hynes understood the weight of the moment, the chance to cement a concept, just as he knew the practical danger of a semifinal hangover. He respected the tight-knit dedication that this squad had developed over two years of playing, training, and living together, yet he feared their adolescence. They sat in that locker room on April 22, buzzing with nervous energy. Coach Hynes stood, arms crossed, the words of his pregame speech caught on his tongue, when the door swung open and in walked Chris Atkinson, sporting a white bandage around his throat.

Fresh from the hospital ward back in the States, a Team USA sweater oddly baggy over his street clothes, Atkinson beamed with vitality as his teammates slapped his back and grinned at him. The tension was shattered. It was a beautiful thing to be young and unstoppable at the World Championships. At long last.

The romance of the moment quickly gave way to a nasty, jarring, shake-your-limbs-loose-from-their-sockets tilt between the boards. The Finns came out tough, boasting a big, bruising, and skilled lineup backed by rock-solid goaltender Riku Helenius, who made a nice save on a Geoffrion backhander to open the game. The adrenaline was pumping, and it was visible on Blake's face, on the faces of his teammates, a jittery energy that had them skating past pucks and in front of passes, missing chances they would normally seize. The Finns' puck movement was crisp and slick. They played a smooth, disciplined game, frustrating the US skaters. Fifteen minutes in, Kane followed up a shot into the glove of Helenius with a little stick tap on his closed mitt, a little showboating to put the Finns in their place. Helenius slammed his stick down in disgust. Things were already edging toward chippy.

Less than nine minutes into the first period, Team USA's Chris Summers, already leading the tournament in penalty minutes, got whistled for tripping, ushering on the Finnish power play, the highest scoring man-advantage unit in the tournament. It was the kind of challenge that Hynes's boys had been taught to relish. Geoffrion and Flynn moved quickly into the neutral zone, gumming up the Finnish attack. They were relentless, fighting for every inch of ice, every second of control in the corners. Team USA successfully killed the penalty but players were still scrambling to regain their footing when a sloppy turnover in front of the US net led to a shot, a rebound, and then a puck on the stick of Joonas Kemppainen, who jammed it past Palmer. 1–0, Finland.

Back in the locker room between periods, Hynes reassured his players in measured tones: "Boys, they're not that good. Do *not* let them dictate the play and the pace. Take a deep breath, get back to our game."

The first period was flatter than it should've been, but forty minutes remained to seek redemption. The players had worked too hard, come too far, to be remembered as the group that lost the gold.

"The Finns are so good at collapsing around their net and not allowing shots of any kind," declared the announcers for the American audience back home, admiration creeping into their voices. For the spectators, it looked like the game was slipping away from Team USA. The view from the ice was different. The Americans believed in their game plan and in their coach. They believed in themselves.

Rhett Rakhshani reset the tone early in the second period, absolutely flattening a Finnish defenseman. The US players refused to be outhustled or outmuscled, and the Finns learned firsthand about the physicality of a team led by John Hynes.

Five minutes into the second period, as Team USA pried open space in the offensive zone, Rakhshani raced across the ice, bumped his defender off his feet, and ripped a shot. Helenius made the save, but Blake captured the rebound and sliced a long shot through the air. Helenius butterflied a save, but the puck kicked out again. Bang, another shot, another save, another rebound, the goalie Helenius now frantic and claustrophobic. Rakhshani, hovering, banged the puck home, leaving the disgusted Finnish goalie to grab it from the back of the cage and fling it at the referee. Tied up, 1–1, thirty-five minutes to play.

Just as the horn signaled the end of the period, Team USA scored a power-play goal to take the lead. Blake's mind raced with the possibilities as the third frame began. As the minutes ticked by, the penalty section of the official scorecard blossomed with ink, a laundry list of bad behavior for both teams. Interference, slashing, tripping, boarding, tripping again. As the action heated up in front of the Finnish net, the players tackled their US counterparts. The scoreboard failed to reflect their rising dominance. "Geoffrion has been snakebitten by Helenius," the announcers exclaimed after yet another crafty shot was stopped by the sizable Finn wedged between the pipes.

Blake shook his head, his cheeks flushed with exertion. His frustration was evident as Jan-Mikael Järvinen lined up for a shot on the US goal, and Blake reached back to hook stick against shin pads and yanked the Finn's legs out from under him. Sitting in the box, wiping his sweat-soaked head with a towel, Blake peered through the Plexiglass as his team went to work to kill two minor penalties in a five-on-three with thirteen minutes remaining in the game. His teammates seemed to be handling the pressure, and only seconds remained on Blake's tripping penalty when all 222 pounds of Erik Johnson exploded into a smaller

Finnish player, sending him headfirst into the boards. The referee and linesmen briefly conferred before Swiss ref Nadir Mandioni pointed a long finger toward the gate, assessing Johnson a game misconduct penalty and ejecting him from the game.

"Fuck!" Johnson was livid, stomping off the ice and shattering his stick against a brick wall. In a game with no room for error, his cheap shot had handcuffed the teammates he had shared the struggle with to get there. A ten-minute major against an elite power-play unit was an eternity.

The US team would have to play the rest of the period down a man. Players bobbed up and down in front of Finnish shooters, flattening sticks, exposing wrists and fingers and thighs to wrist shots as the penalty kill dragged on. Jamie McBain took one to the chest and groaned his way off the ice. Michael Carman was right behind him, dragging a leg. Blood and bruises marked the passage of time. Blake was everywhere, tossing bodies off pucks, laying out, disrupting rushes, then back on the bench, shaking his right arm and grimacing in pain.

Seven minutes to go.

Tucked off the ice, two gray-haired men polished a dazzling trophy. The white-helmeted players who raced and darted and dived were laser-focused on the puck, but their eyes occasionally peeked at the clock.

Three minutes to go.

Erik Johnson watched, arms folded, standing in his street clothes on the other side of the glass next to a stoic Chris Atkinson.

Two minutes to go.

Team Finland pulled its goalie, adding a sixth player to its attack. Yet Palmer turned away one try after another.

Forty-five seconds, twenty, ten, five, Mike Carman lunged and smashed a puck out of the zone, watched it glide across the center line and down the ice into the back of the empty Finnish net. Two dozen young men piled onto their goaltender, gloves and hats littering the ice behind them. Palmer was spinning like a top, screaming with glee. Never mind that there were two seconds left on the clock and the referee had to skate over to a grinning Coach Hynes to demand his players clear the ice.

It didn't matter. They had won the gold medal. This was their time. For some, it would be the purest hockey joy they'd ever know.

As the national anthem boomed, the players stood in a line, tears streaming and skates shuffling, gold medals draped around their necks. Then the young men retreated to the locker room, where they stood arm in arm, wailing the lyrics to "We Are the Champions" as members of an off-key choir. In the showers, still giddy with excitement despite the checkerboard of bruises etched across their bodies, they laughed and recounted the big hits and the toughest blocks until Atkinson, still wearing his jersey and khakis, charged in, prompting peals of mirth from his teammates. The next day, they boarded the plane back to the States, swinging through their billet homes in Michigan to thank their hosts of two years and to grab their personal effects before heading to their homes in Bloomington, Minnesota; Waltham, Massachusetts; Huntington Beach, California; Brentwood, Tennessee.

All the while, the words of Coach Hynes rung in their ears: Champions walk together forever.

"From the day you arrive at Team USA, the whole time, it's about the medals," recalled Blake. Before the plane had even landed, his mom had already ordered a frame big enough to hold a national team jersey and a shiny new gold medal right above it.

chapter 3

FINDING WISCONSIN

I n the Kohl Center, home of the Wisconsin Badgers men's ice hockey team, there hangs a banner brilliant in its whiteness, edged in vivid cardinal red, overlooking a gleaming sheet of ice. The iconic words of Bob Johnson, the founding father of the Badger program, are spelled out across its center, inviting one and all to join below: "It's a great day for hockey."

The quote is sweet, almost mocking in its simplicity, offering a welcoming gesture to anyone who would like to watch or perhaps even skate a shift or two. Its words seem better suited to the grace of a round of golf or croquet, pastimes whose participants don't regularly lose their teeth or lower a shoulder and smash their opponents into the nearest wall.

"A great day for hockey" is deceptive, however, implying a pleasantness absent from a hockey rink even in the most joyful moments of the game. Sweat regularly splatters across the ice, mixing with the blood of broken noses and gashed mouths and eyebrows and chins, regular occurrences in even the friendliest of matchups, symptoms of the sport's obsession with speed. The game's central object, a disk of hard black rubber flung at players with crippling velocity, makes no distinction between friend and foe, stick and cartilage and bone. Thousands seeking renown have skated under Badger Bob's words; only a few of those skaters have achieved it—the heroes of Wisconsin hockey: Andringa and Skille, Heatley and Richter, Eaves and Johnson, Pavelski, Chelios, and Suter. And Geoffrion.

The Kohl Center sits on the corner of West Dayton and North Frances Streets in Madison, built of gray stone and shimmering blue glass, gazing benevolently at the fans marching up its frozen steps and into one of its enticing entrances. It is named after Herb Kohl, the department store magnate turned US senator who wrote the check for the arena's primary funding, to the tune of $25 million, in the late 1990s. It has served as home to the Badgers' men's hockey and men's and women's basketball teams ever since they moved over from the old Dane County Coliseum. Since its opening in 1998, the rink has become the backdrop for enduring Badger sports lore, from Dany Heatley's dazzling four-point night against Michigan Tech in March 2002 to Brian Elliott's awe-inspiring performances, weekend after weekend, during the magical spring of 2006, when the Badgers chased their sixth national championship trophy. Some years, the Badgers' home arena has averaged more fans per game than the NHL's Chicago Blackhawks have drawn to the United Center.

But the man who opened the door to possibility, who took a fledgling program and turned it into a perennial powerhouse on the college hockey national stage, never set foot inside the building. Laboring away at the Dane County Coliseum, Johnson breathed life into a sport once relegated to Wisconsin's outdoor rinks and third-tier conferences. In all its off-campus splendor, the coliseum's walls had absorbed an affinity for the game so deep and abiding that friends, adversaries, referees, and sportswriters, Wisconsin natives and Minnesota transplants alike, came to respect it as *the* place to play the game. One Western Collegiate Hockey Association (WCHA) referee called it the "Montreal Forum of college hockey."

For a sport whose north star hangs above the banks of the St. Lawrence River, there could be no greater compliment.

When the Badgers played at the coliseum, it was a magical, suds-soaked palace—conveniently located off campus, the arena housed a beer hall that summoned new fans as powerfully as the teams themselves—

a ring of blue and white carnival stripes just below the roof that welcomed patrons to the festive atmosphere with the promise of warmth and camaraderie and intoxication. Once inside, the first jostled shoulder or, heaven forbid, glimpse of a University of Minnesota Golden Gopher offered a sobering reminder that patrons had come for a higher purpose than drinking.

Wisconsin hired Bob Johnson as head coach in 1966, a year before the team began playing in the coliseum, and his hockey evangelism soon won over the masses. Fans came with souls that needed feeding and hands reddened by the cold, gesticulating wildly at the unfortunates who slated to play the Badgers. Johnson was a master coach, adept at assembling a loose collection of smooth high school faces into a ruthless, efficient, scoring, checking, passing machine and racking up wins in college hockey's toughest conference at a blistering pace. The fans, bored with losing football and basketball teams and perennially facing the prospect of another long, gray winter, thirsted for more—for wins, for fights, for open-ice checks and dropped gloves and championships. Bob had turned on the tap. He wouldn't stop serving up success for another twelve years.

College hockey rose to new heights in the 1970s and 1980s on the shoulders of two titans, Badger Bob Johnson and the University of Minnesota's Herb Brooks. The two men urged their chosen combatants ever onward, Gopher and Badger skaters colliding mere feet away as the coaches stood watching, resisting the urge to glance sideways through the thin sheet of Plexiglass at the other man. Johnson coached his teams to national championships in '73, '77, and '81, taking 1976 off to coach the US Olympic team in Innsbruck, Austria. Brooks's teams collected titles in '74, '76, and '79 before he succeeded Johnson as the head coach for Team USA for the Winter Olympics in Lake Placid, taking Badger Bob's son Mark with him.

What is it about hockey that sends midwesterners into a frenzy? No one holds a grudge like family, and no argument is more heated than a clash between siblings over a Thanksgiving table. Too similar to be easily differentiated, too proud to admit it, brothers and sisters look for any outlet to reignite old resentments and jockey for position within the familial hierarchy. The states of the Upper Midwest share borders, cultural heritage, the peculiar intonation of their *O*s, and a penchant for passive aggressiveness. They are nothing if not siblings. Carrying grudges silently like so many stones in their pockets, midwesterners have designated the hockey rink as the one place in their world where it is acceptable to hate.

And hate they did. And do. After Minnesota hoisted the NCAA trophy in 1976, it was whispered in Madison that Brooks had held back his best players from the Johnson-coached US Olympic squad, an unpatriotic and unpardonable sin. Brooks, in turn, sniped at Johnson in the press, accusing his rival of passing over Gopher players when constructing the Team USA lineup four years later. The fall of 1976, when their collegiate clashes resumed, Brooks had to be restrained from shoving a heckling fan against a coliseum wall. Johnson was presumably out of reach.

The better the teams, the more vitriolic the rivalries. Wisconsin returned to the Frozen Four in 1978, losing to the eventual champion Boston University Terriers at Rhode Island's Providence Civic Center. Minnesota took the trophy in 1979. North Dakota won in '80, but Wisconsin triumphed again in '81, defeating Minnesota. Despite the Badger victory, Minnesota's Neal Broten received the inaugural Hobey Baker Award, given to the top NCAA men's ice hockey player. The honor was named after "America's most romantic athlete," a Princeton University hockey star who had been killed in a fighter plane crash hours before he was due to return to the United States from France at the end of World War I.[1] The award recognized both on-ice achievements and office character—that combination of talent, leadership, humility, and character that separates the iconic from the merely memorable. For college hockey fans, so often bitter about their little-brother status on the stage next to football and basketball, the award also came to symbolize the one moment every year when the spotlight was theirs and theirs alone.

Watching the bronze statue loaded onto the Gopher team bus that first year was a bitter pill for Badger fans to swallow.

North Dakota took the championship in '82, beating Wisconsin 5–2, but the Badgers won again the next year with Johnson's former assistant Jeff Sauer holding the reins. It was a period of dominant parity nearly unrivaled in North American team sports. From then on, future Badger captains from Steve Rohlik to Blake Geoffrion carried the dual burden of tradition and expectation.

Many recall the ferocity of the Bruins–Canadiens enmity in the 1970s NHL or dream wistfully of the Celtics–Lakers saga of the NBA in the 1980s. But the professional rivalries, remarkable in their own way, are bought and paid for, proof of purchase on the back of the box. Their stars, plucked from the ranks of thousands, are brands unto themselves, drawn to the fan bases by the forces of the free market and the vagaries of the draft. Players may bemoan trades away from cities of which they've grown fond, but there's a new address on their paycheck, and it won't pick itself up from the team secretary.

The sheer domination of three college hockey teams—the Golden Gophers, the Fighting Sioux (later changed to the Fighting Hawks), and the Badgers—over the course of a decade was made even more remarkable by the fact that their programs were assembled not on a spreadsheet with a column for dollar signs but around a 1,001 kitchen tables, with coaches relying on rigor and charisma to attract talent and then wring every drop of it from the young men who had bought what the coaches were selling. No free agent acquisitions could plug holes in a lineup—develop or die, haunted always by the ticking clock of eligibility.

To win it once in a decade was remarkable. Twice was meteoric. More? You've got to be kidding.

"They knew they had to go through each other to win a national championship," said Brad Schlossman, UND hockey beat writer for the *Grand Forks Herald*. "If your teams are bad, nobody really cares."

∽

In a low-slung brick building that hugs the concrete curb along Langdon Street, bracing itself against the chill of the wind blowing across the lake next door, lives a scene that is both unremarkable and unlike any other. To outsiders, it seems an indistinct college drinking establishment, littered with the lumpy booth benches and beer pong tables that come standard with any college watering hole. But to the undergraduates of Madison, it's a palace.

This particular bar exerts magnetic forces on student-athletes and their admirers. All the jocks who walk through the door are wound tight with the headiness of their own campus celebrity, just as they are equally unsettled by the knowledge that their athletic eligibility is fleeting, and with it someday soon will go the splendor of *just existing* in a place like this!

The Kollege Klub is "Where Kollegians Kongregate." Under the influence of a shot and a beer (the former comes free with the latter on Wednesday nights), the edges of the room may grow fuzzy as inhibitions plummet. Have another round, and it becomes clear why hockey players, recruits, alumni, and admirers have been stumbling through the KK's doors since 1953.

Playboy magazine, in crafting its famous annual party-school ranking lists, once left off UW–Madison, stating that "it would be unfair to rank professionals with the amateurs." For collegians suddenly thrust into the sporting spotlight, the town was rife with temptation.

"When I got there, the culture was 'get to the bar on time,'" remembered Adam Burish, a winger who joined the Badger program as a freshman in the fall of 2002. Burish was a Madison native, and all of his hockey heroes were Badgers. As a tween, he dreamed not of the NHL and a chance to hoist the Stanley Cup but of a national championship won wearing Wisconsin red and white, the lofty strains of "Varsity" echoing down State Street, a crowd of fans on hand to celebrate the mightiest of Madison hockey achievements.

In prior eras, a spot on the UW squad might have been the closest thing to a guarantee of winning a national title. But college hockey was not immune to changing tides. Jeff Sauer had taken over for his mentor, Bob Johnson, in 1982 and led the team to a national championship the following year and again in 1990. The Badgers returned to the national title game in 1992, only to lose to tiny Lake Superior State—the last Sauer-led team to play for a championship ring.

By the early 2000s, the program was adrift. The 2001–2 Badgers finished with a sub-.500 record following the departure of goal-scoring wizard Dany Heatley for the NHL the year before. Sauer's looseness with his players, a style that had served him so admirably for years, was failing to produce the results fans expected.

He retired as head coach in the spring of 2002, and chatter in the Madison taverns held to the conventional wisdom that Mark Johnson, 1980 Olympic hero and the son of Badger Bob, would ascend to his rightful place on the throne. But such monarchical elevation was not meant to be. Instead, University of Wisconsin athletic director Pat Richter called Johnson's old linemate Mike Eaves, fresh off a gold-medal win at the U18 World Championships, and invited him to come home to Madison.

～

"As a new coach, you want to establish what you feel is a winning culture," Mike Eaves said.

Eaves and his new assistant, John Hynes, also poached from the National Team Development Program, were determined to construct a culture that relied on rigorous adhesion to conditioning paired with personal accountability. This approach frequently left his players kneeling in pools of their own sweat far from the ice on which they'd been recruited to play.

The new coach found out that some of his players were dogging their postpractice cooldowns and took it upon himself to don a sweatsuit and run with them, through the snow if need be, a near-fifty-year-old with the fires of competition still burning in his icy blue eyes.

On that team, in that year, *everyone* was going to skate—and run and lift and wrestle on the football turf—until they dropped. Before the school year had even started, strict standards were set. Anything more than 10 percent body fat would result in a benching, regardless of skill. Eaves and Hynes instituted a rigid 10/10 test—players had to run on a 10 percent incline at ten miles per hour until they fell off the treadmill. Anyone who wanted to start needed to beat the team average.

"If you wanted to play at Wisconsin, you needed to be above average," recalled Adam Burish. "Our best defenseman, who had just beaten cancer, ran two seconds short. And Eaves said, 'You're not playing. I'm sorry.'" True to his promise, Eaves kept him out of the starting lineup.

Burish, a freshman, had expected college hockey to be tough, anticipating a fitness program that would leave his muscles bulging and his skinny high school physique a distant memory. Eaves's program seemed borderline sadistic. A. J. Degenhart, another freshman, passed out cold after a five-mile run in the August heat, and trainers rushed to attend to his unconscious body.[2]

As the temperature fell, each player was forced to carry a partner on his back for one hundred yards at full sprint across frozen pavement with hockey socks wrapped around their ears for warmth. These hellish scenes had been conspicuously omitted from all of those kitchen-table recruiting conversations.

One by one, Sauer's recruits quit or were cut, unwilling to bend under the ferocity of the new system. Eaves demanded as much of his players on the ice as off it, pressing his blueliners into a forechecking intensity that had been anathema to Sauer's stay-at-home defensive style. Eaves coached as he had played, demanding a battle over every inch, never conceding, leading by example until the sweat dripped from his own brow. He instituted a curfew—long before bar time. In his first season at the helm of a dynasty hockey program, Mike Eaves wasn't taking any chances.

Especially with a bunch of college kids. Especially in a town like that.

Thirteen wins.

Through the 2002–3 season, Eaves's team scraped together just thirteen wins in forty games, an ominous start to a tenure that had begun so optimistically, so boldly confident in the face of boosters' grumbling.

Nevertheless, he recruited. In those early years, much of the young talent was coming off the frozen ponds and gently groomed rinks of the Badger State itself.

Ryan Suter, a Madison native, was starting to show all the signs of his Miracle-on-Ice pedigree as a budding defenseman. Jack Skille, another child of an Eaves teammate from the '77 team and a local product, grabbed every inch of ice that Davis Drewiskie from Hudson, Wisconsin, could muscle free for him. And Joe Pavelski was hailed as the Polish Prince, the Pride of Plover, a mere hundred miles from the shiny new Kohl Center.

With each passing year, Eaves added new bricks to his program's foundation, recruiting for size, speed, skill, brains, and brawn. When his recruiting efforts took him outside Wisconsin, he found himself returning, time and time again, to the fertile ground of the NTDP. Hynes had returned to coach the U17 team and made sure to keep his former boss apprised of the talent ripe for picking. Eaves couldn't be at every U17 game, but then again, he didn't need to be. All he had to do was reach out to Hynes, his old assistant, and he'd hear exactly which of the seventeen-year-olds possessed the right stuff. Two names stood out: Jamie McBain on the blue line, and that tall kid with the famous last name, Blake Geoffrion, up front. Team USA had become a magnet for the very best. The well was deep, and his thirst was unquenchable.

Unlike the typical highly touted prospect who comes out of a traditional hockey state and is nearly impossible to lure away from the local big-time program and regular opportunities play in front of friends and family every weekend, Blake was a true free agent, a recruiter's dream, with no family ties to a program whose coach could flash a friendly grin, drape an arm across the young man's shoulders, and make some soapy pitch about following his daddy's skates and joining the mighty whoevers.

The University of Denver pursued Blake in earnest, watching his dimensions grow and his mettle blossom under the tutelage of the NTDP coaches. Miami University in Ohio and Boston University were there, too, as was Red Berenson, the legendary Michigan coach who had added two national championship trophies to the case in Ann Arbor during the '90s.

"Make sure you get this guy," Eaves rasped in the ear of Burish, the Badgers' captain and most dependable recruit closer. Burish was bombastic and brash, but he was serious when it came to two things: scoring goals and selling Madison. He excelled at both. The tradition depended on it.

Burish was used to pointing out the splendor of the classic campus, reminding his charges of the five national championships and of the numerous program alumni who had gone on to the NHL and then smugly shepherding the recruits to the Kollege Klub, confident in another commitment secured and a job well done. The beauty of the campus and the romance of its hockey history, washed down with a few cold beers and a shot or two, was usually more than enough to close the deal. But the tall, loquacious prospect from Tennessee wasn't going to let Burish off nearly so easily.

Seated at the KK bar, a beer sweating, forgotten, on the polished wood before him, Blake peppered Burish with questions. What were the coaches like? How did they like to recruit, and who else were they targeting? What kind of work ethic did they believe in? Did players practice in the summer? Were the fans as loud, as ferocious, as educated about hockey as he'd heard? Why had it been so long since their last championship? Did everyone want to win as badly as he did? The winning, Burish assured him, was already underway. He and his teammates were marching toward their second consecutive NCAA tournament appearance. The junior captain had fully bought into the program he had been tasked with selling to recruits—even this recruit, who probed each claim with a skepticism that bordered on insolence. Burish spat scorn at the mention of other schools and gesticulated wildly, emphatically, hammering home his points over and over: this was the place for players who wanted to win national championships, become the best, learn what they needed to know to become more than just a draft pick with promise.

Blake had originally been inclined toward Michigan, retaining a fondness for the maize-striped helmets he'd so admired on ESPN back in Brentwood, and he'd said as much to Berenson on his official recruiting visit earlier that fall. Blake's forty-eight-hours on the Madison campus had left a lingering impression, though.

Back on the ice with Team USA a few weeks after his chat with Burish, Blake couldn't shake the nagging pull west toward the Badger State. The Madison salesman had spoken the magic words: rich history and contemporary contention, team chemistry and personal growth; skills development, school pride, leadership that could produce a captain of that caliber; an excellent education, on the ice and off it, in a picture-perfect setting on the Lake Mendota shoreline. Wisconsin wanted him badly, yes, and didn't take him for granted, but he wouldn't be coddled if he chose to play for Eaves.

Red Berenson was a giant who had led two teams to national championships in the 1990s. He had also played with Boom Boom Geoffrion in the NHL, a fact of which he hadn't needed to remind Blake on his tour of the University of Michigan campus. The Wolverine coach had every reason to feel assured that the young center would choose the maize and blue, a confidence Blake could feel through the phone during their next conversation.

"Hey, Blake, do you want to come over and sign that deal?"

"Red, I need to think a little more about this one."

"What the hell do you mean?"

Blake mumbled that he would call back again soon. When he did, he confessed that he had done all the thinking he needed.

"Coach, I've decided to play for Wisconsin."

The phone went dead.

∼

Mike Eaves had his center of the future. But Blake still had another year of high school to finish, another year to play with the NTDP, and Wisconsin needed help for the 2005–6 season. Eaves really needed a skill player, a net-finding fiend who could get and pad the lead when things got desperate in the march through the WCHA gauntlet and into the NCAA tournament. If he could fill one more spot with the glimmer of offensive wizardry, the Badgers would be the preseason favorites to win it all in the campaign to come.

Eaves didn't even have to fill up his gas tank to find his wizard. Phil Kessel was a born-and-bred Madison west-sider. His parents had been Wisconsin hockey season ticket holders for years. Bob Suter had coached Kessel, and Dany Heatley had dazzled the boy since his Pee Wee days.

All Eaves thought he had to do was ask.

~

The commonly accepted method for five-star recruits to publicly announce their college commitments used to be fairly simple. A young man would sit at a table with a row of hats bearing school logos in front of him and family and friends clustered around. With cameras and microphones from local and national media outlets arrayed before him, he would smile, announce his pride in joining the program at such and such a university, then don the appropriate hat. By the early twenty-first century, the top emerging basketball and football players had come to expect this level of attention, but not until March 4, 2005, did ESPN, the Worldwide Leader in Sports, carry its first live hockey commitment. Reporters had come to the NTDP's headquarters in Ann Arbor, Michigan, to hear where Phil Kessel would play his college hockey. Two hats sat before him on the table: Minnesota and Wisconsin.

Badger fans were giddy with excitement. Already a household name in his hometown, Kessel seemed destined to bring UW fans their sixth championship.

Until his extended hand closed around the corn-yellow cap with a maroon *M*. *M* for Minnesota. Wisconsin's finest-ever hockey prospect was headed north to be a Gopher.

From that moment, the entire college hockey world focused on the weekend of January 27, 2006, when Kessel would return to Madison and make his Kohl Center debut in enemy colors. Among those paying attention would be Blake and others playing out their final year with the NTDP, the start to their college careers just over the horizon.

"He wasn't tough enough to play in Wisconsin. Minnesota boys are prima donnas," the Badgers told each other.

The locker-room chatter and the postpractice growling ratcheted up with every passing day, so blinding the Wisconsin skaters with rivalry rage that Kessel was, for the first and last time, labeled a card-carrying pretty boy. Tickets, already in short supply around campus as the Badgers rode the first-place spot in the national college hockey rankings for the seventh consecutive week, disappeared.

"Sold Out, Sold Out," proclaimed signs above the Kohl Center ticket offices, raising goose bumps on the muscled arms of the players entering the arena. All of the arena's 15,237 seats were filled for Friday night's game, filled with spectators primed with a special kind of loathing reserved for the Benedict Arnold of college hockey. The fans felt personally spurned, brides left waiting at the altar.

"It's Minni Week, it's Minni Week . . ." A staccato thumping of the border battle war drums rose from the Wisconsin alumni, the 1990 national champion team especially vocal in reminding the current players of the tradition they had inherited. The players became livid. Some would stay angry long after the final whistle was blown. "Even when I was in the NHL," said Burish, "I still hated Minnesota."

Wisconsin's star goalie, Hobey Baker finalist Brian Elliott, was out with an injury, and from first line to fourth line, starters and pine riders all understood how damn good they needed to be.

On Friday night, they weren't good enough. The Badgers lost, 4–3.

A mass of humanity surged through the gates on Saturday, salivating for a chance to make their views known. Eighteen players, clad tip to toe in maroon and gold, stood on the red paint of the end line, already scraped dull by thirty-six skates shuffling nervously back and forth. The loudspeakers boomed as the announcer began to introduce the Minnesota players: "No. 34, the goaltender . . ."

The name was cut off as the crowd erupted, chopping their arms and pointing as they chanted *Sieve! Sieve! Sieve!* This relentless hectoring of opposing netminders had been a Madison staple for decades; this evening, it radiated white hot, Badger fans flinging every ounce of loathing they could muster at the opposing team. The national anthem eventually calmed the watching thousands, leaving them gulping for air, a brief respite before the puck smacked onto the ice.

Three minutes and forty-four seconds later, Adam Burish found Robbie Earl, who fed the puck to Tom Gilbert. Minnesota's Ben Gordon watched helplessly from the penalty box, the red lights of the goal lamp dancing across his face, as the Badgers took a 1–0 lead. Again the crowd boomed its medieval dirge: *Sieve! Sieve! Sieve!*

This time the students added a new chant: "Fu-uck Kessel! Fu-uck Kessel!"

Police officers quickly shuffled through the student section, hushing the profane, but they could do nothing to suppress the boos that rained down from every seat in the house each time Kessel touched the puck. The members of the crowd were so fixated on jeering this ungrateful whelp all the way back across the state line, seemingly oblivious that Wisconsin had let in two goals and given away the lead, that they seemed caught by surprise, voices trapped in their throats for an instant, when Kessel snared a feed at center ice, rocked the puck back into a dirty little dangle, and then flung a wrister past the backup Badger goalie, freshman Shane Connelly. A stunned silence hung for a fraction of a second, until Kessel cupped his ear in an "I can't hear youuuuuuu" gesture, bringing them howling back to life. Amid the boos, the villain leapt into the embrace of his hooting teammates. Seven minutes later, the Gophers joyfully collided again, having clinched their 3–1 victory.

The Badgers muddled through the rest of the month, splitting back-to-back series, before dropping an embarrassing pair of losses to lowly Minnesota State–Mankato. The team's leaders were furious with themselves and with their linemates.

Burish assured Eaves that the players would handle the situation. Relinquishing control was uncharacteristic for the coach, particularly after watching this team squander an eight-point lead in the conference standings. But something in his captain's eyes and in his determined tone told Eaves that his boys had earned a new level of trust. And once the locker room door clicked shut, the dressing down began, a condemnation of shirked responsibility so intense it threatened to peel the paint from the walls.

"They wanted the reins. And they rode that pony all the way to the championship," Eaves said.

The Badgers closed out the regular season with a pair of victories over St. Cloud State and then bounced Michigan Tech from the WCHA tournament. Though they lost to North Dakota in the tourney's semifinals, they recorded a satisfying 4–0 trouncing of Minnesota, in Minneapolis, in the third-place game, in their final game before the NCAA tournament. Through sixty dominant minutes, Phil Kessel was held without a point.

A week later, Joe Pavelski tallied a hat trick against an overmatched Bemidji State in a first-round NCAA tournament game held in Green Bay, practically home ice for the Badgers. Next up was Cornell, with a berth in the Frozen Four on the line.

Cornell and Wisconsin held each other scoreless through three periods and two overtimes. By the third extra session, players were skating listlessly past each other, pushing the puck from end to end, weaving, wavering, the rubber disk an anvil against their sticks.

Fans rubbed their eyes like tired toddlers. Each player skated on, hating his own existence, wanting it all to end. Somehow, drawing from the deepest reserves, Josh Engel flipped a weary backhand pass across to Jack Skille, who gathered it, wound up, and slapped it by the goalie.

"Oh baby, it's been a long time, Wisconsin fans!" crowed the announcer.

Blake Geoffrion, watching from his billet home in Michigan, crowed right back. Seventy-one minutes of grit and grind had confirmed what he had already known: Wisconsin was the place for him. Mike Eaves's team could outskill and outhustle and could win when it mattered. After fourteen years, the Badgers were headed back to the Frozen Four.

Down Interstate 94 the team bus rolled, the exuberance of the human cargo trapped inside bubbling up with each passing mile, each minute distant from the three overtimes. What to do now? The wonder of a national championship berth had them reinvigorated—and restless. Burish called Tom Sagissor, captain of the '90 team, for championship counsel.

"What have you guys done all year?" asked Sagissor.

Well, they'd gone out after games, naturally, to the Kollege Klub, to hold court and rehydrate with beer.

"Then you're going out tonight! Try not to drink everything."

Eleven days later, Burish and his teammates rolled through the University of Maine Black Bears, 5–2, and secured their place in the national championship game against Boston College.

⌒

Kkllaang! Mike Eaves would never forget that sound as long as he lived.

Down in the first period, then tied, then in tenuous possession of a 2–1 lead after Tom Gilbert scored from the slot following a raucous, Van Halen–fueled second intermission, Eaves found that his pursuit of glory—for himself, his players, his alma mater, and his coaching legacy—came down to a scrum in the final seconds of the third period. The Boston College skaters were swarming the net, leaving Brian Elliott scrambling, thrusting his stick between legs, willing the puck to stay out of the goal's ravenous mouth.

That sound—the puck ringing off the post—jarred Eaves. Had the puck kicked in? He stared at the referee as the buzzer sounded. Players smashed in a group hug, relief spilling free, net knocked off its moorings. No coaches joined in. They stared transfixed at the referee, holding their breath, until the signal came: No goal!

Eaves joined the melee, skittering in dress shoes across the rink to hug his players. The Badgers had won. Yet another championship trophy would take its place in the Kohl Center. Ever the dignified competitor, Eaves quickly extracted himself to grip the hand of BC's Jerry York and accept his congratulations.

"It was our turn. It was our turn."

chapter 4

CHASING THE HOBEY

Rubber pucks smacking into plastic walls at tremendous speeds cause a hammer strike to the eardrums that makes the heart leap and sends a thousand splinters of electricity pulsing into the gut. Not so much a *crack!* as a *ffwwuuuuApp!*, a gunpowder-charged report echoing through the closed confines of an arena. It takes a real boomer of a slap shot to generate that sound, to threaten the structural integrity of the seemingly resolute rink boards, to cause a half-second pause in the minds of defensemen poised to leap into the path of the next shot, to send cold perspiration bursting from the pores of a goaltender, drenching his pads.

Austin Lee stood tall in goal, sweating. A slapper had just sailed by his head with stomach-turning velocity and *ffwwuuuuApp*ed the boards loud enough to elicit an embarrassing flinch from the senior. Blinking through salty eyes, he watched a hulking figure in red and white skate away from him. No. 5. *Geoffrion . . .*

Mike Eaves was not amused.

As Blake Geoffrion clambered back onto the bench, skates click-clacking against the half wall, Eaves leaned forward and bellowed down the line of seated players. "Take that slap shot outta your game!"

A vein popped out along his neck. They knew he was serious. And Blake, ever dutiful, ever coachable, hung his head . . . but not quite low enough to hide the grin beaming through his helmet cage.

Another forty-five seconds ticked by, and Blake was over the boards again, scooping up a clean pass, then off to the races down the left side, past a glowering Eaves, slowing just inside the blue line. Blake wound up, struck the puck, and launched it on a blistering path over Lee's left shoulder.

The chilled air was rent open by the blast of the horn and the screams of his fans. They whooped and howled as big No. 5 skated back to the bench and pointed, grinning delightedly, at his coach.

All Eaves could do was point back, grinning himself. There was too much of Boom Boom Geoffrion in Blake's blood. Eaves had to give his captain a little line to run with.

$\sim$

Boom Boom's grandson.

He might have been a relentless student of the game, obsessed with studying tape and watching highlights and chronicling stat books, but a romantic streak ran through Blake, now twenty-two years old and in his senior year at the University of Wisconsin. His grandfather had invented the slap shot, thrilling crowds and terrifying goalies with sudden and searing power. The shot might have faded from popularity as the game tightened up, leaving fewer opportunities for the necessary windup, but that night, in front of an adoring crowd fully invested to this latest chapter in the Geoffrion saga, the slap shot was experiencing a revival.

"The slap shot is a glamorous thing, the way it was," Maple Leafs coach Ron Wilson reminisced. "A guy coming down the wing, letting one fly. It was like a towering home run in baseball. There's nothing like it when a guy hits one of those majestic home runs—the ones where you just say, 'Wow.'"

Some students of hockey claim that minor leaguer George Ouellette beat Boom Boom to the punch, developing the slap shot a few years earlier, but, then again, as one reporter put it, "no sportswriter ever thought to call him Boom Boom."

Sports nicknames can bestow instant legend even the most forgettable athlete—ask any second-rate boxer who rode the elevator of good publicity to the A-side of a fight card with the help of a clever moniker.

More often, though, it cements a great player into the collective memory of a fan base. Every Minnesotan worth his lutefisk knows the Purple People Eaters. No member of the Trio Grande line will have to pay for his own beer on Long Island anytime soon. Boom Boom's hockey exploits were still required reading for schoolchildren in Quebec.

~

"His sixteenth goal of the season, scored by No. Five, Blake Geoff-ri-ooooooon!"

The loudspeakers blared, and fifteen thousand Badger fans peered gleefully upward as Blake's irreverent slap shot goal played out again across the Jumbotron. Now in his fourth season at Wisconsin, with dozens of collegiate goals under his belt, Blake had become a topic of kitchen table conversation for hockey fans across the state, and he hadn't needed a clever nickname to get there. He was simply "Blake."

It was February 12, 2010. The Badgers' tally so far this season: seventeen wins, seven losses, and four ties; two rumored Hobey Baker candidates in Geoffrion, he of the screaming slap shot and thirty total points, and Brendan Smith, the junior blue-line sensation out of Ontario who seemed to score every time Blake didn't. Wisconsin had produced seven Hobey Baker finalists over the preceding three decades. None had brought the award back to Madison.

The Badgers had started the weekend ranked No. 3 nationally after defeating No. 19 ranked Michigan in front of fifty-five thousand fans, outdoors in subzero temperatures, the weekend before. This team was an eternity removed from where it had sat after opening weekend of the 2009–10 college hockey season, Blake's final year of NCAA eligibility: unranked and winless, with two of their best players—Smith and Michael Davies—both healthy scratches to begin the season.

Now, nearly four months later, Blake was brimming with confidence. Gone was the brashness of an overgrown freshman. The red captain's *C* rested comfortably on his shoulder, a superfluous reminder of leader status earned, painstakingly, one lesson at a time. On the road, in the gym, during summer workouts and dawn-broken practices. In Madison.

~

Four years earlier, when the *Wisconsin State Journal* had reported Blake's commitment—"Grandson of NHL Legend Bernie 'Boom Boom' Geoffrion Will Join UW in 2006"—Madisonians quickly rushed to brush up on their Quebecois hockey history.

Bernie Geoffrion's name might have been unfamiliar, but *Boom Boom* had a magical quality to it. The unenlightened might have found Blake's family history a generation further back even more compelling: Great-grandson of the Babe Ruth of Hockey? The defending national champions were practically getting a legend in the making.

Beginning in 2004, the NHL and the NCAA had agreed to let eighteen-year-old players be taken in the NHL Entry Draft without forfeiting their college eligibility. A team could draft a player, retain his rights through four years of college, and then opt to sign him when he decided to turn pro. The new rule allowed NHL teams to watch from afar as their prospects (they hoped) blossomed under collegiate tutelage, although the urge to meddle could be difficult to resist.

The Nashville Predators had traded away their first-round pick in the 2006 entry draft. When their turn came, halfway through the second round, Blake Geoffrion was still on the board, and David Poile didn't hesitate. Nashville's president of operations and general manager had already decided to bring the Tennessee native home as soon as he was ready. Blake thus moved into his on-campus apartment in Madison not just as an international gold medalist but also as an NHL draft pick and future hometown hero. It was enough to go to the head of even the most grounded eighteen-year-old.

The hype bubbled up to a boil as Blake's freshman season approached in the fall of 2006, with the local CBS station even airing a spot, "Ice Runs in His Blood," complete with an acoustic soundtrack pilfered from a Hallmark movie and a voice-over recitation of his impeccable breeding like that of a racetrack announcer.

All the press attention and fan intrigue were tinged by a sense of inevitability. Anyone who carried that name must be marching toward greatness. This blessed storyline glossed over an inconvenient truth.

Blake was one generation removed from hockey celebrity. Danny's draft bust had relegated him to the role of steward of the family story. On camera for CBS, Danny sat squarely, ever the proud father, reciting tales of the hockey heroism of his father and grandfather. It would fall to his son, though, to prove that excellence could be more than just a memory.

In the words of Blake's Pappy, he who wanted to score the goals had to shoot the puck. Blake needed to find the back of the net.

College hockey has a tendency toward hard landings for those entering straight from secondary school, stripping away the varnish of even the most polished prospects. Unlike basketball and football, collegiate hockey does not rely solely on a steady diet of eighteen-year-olds pilfered directly from the shelves of the prep sports supermarket.

The skilled players who do enter college programs directly out of high school find themselves across the face-off circle from older players who have skated for a year or two or three in the Canadian major junior leagues before enrolling. Those players are bigger, stronger, and tougher, with the muscle mass and grit borne of seasons spent grinding through games in little industrial towns on both sides of the US-Canadian border. As a result, the average age of a college hockey freshman is almost 20.5, and a few are even as old as 21. Staring across at a baby-faced eighteen-year-old smitten with his own press attention, those veterans might well be tempted to try to grind off a little of that glimmer.

Immature. Arrogant. Entitled. Bigheaded. Pigheaded. Any of those adjectives could have been applied to Blake that first season on campus. "I was an asshole, to be honest with you," he recalled.

Blake was a walking, talking underclassman stereotype, an entitled chatterbox with an opinion about everything. His was a game heavy on arrogance but light on offensive production. The gold medal he had collected with Team USA had swelled his self-importance. So had the media hype, first around the draft and then when he arrived in

Madison. He talked incessantly—in the locker room, at practice, when visiting upperclassmen's apartments, during team workouts. He chirped at opponents and teammates alike. Even his fastest teammates couldn't outskate the Geoffrion chatter.

As a freshman, Blake was as unremarkable in appearance as he was in his play. Six-foot-two—tall but not out of the ordinary. A muscular 195 pounds, well-built but not imposing. Medium-brown hair framed a wholesome face, but he was not the pretty-boy winger of enduring stereotype. Even when he pursed his lips to hide his boyish smile, he looked the part of the forgettable freshman, just one more in a crowd of teenagers new to campus.

Bob Lindauer, Steamfitters Local 601, Madison, Wisconsin, was there to help Blake move into his dorm. He had been around the Badger program for decades and knew the type as well as any coach—and better than some. Back when Lindauer had begun following the program in the 1970s, Badger hockey had been carried on not one but two radio stations, with Paul Braun doing the play-by-play on WIBA 1310 AM and Bob Miller and Chuck Kaiton handling the mike for WTSO 1070. Lindauer had kept stat books, shuttled errant freshmen around town, and dispensed advice with a friendly grin. Once, in the middle of a blizzard, he had dug the players' cars out of the snow even before their plane had touched back down after a road series. He could sense Blake's natural ability to lead even through all that brashness.

Cocky became Blake's accidental calling card. At one party in the apartment of a few older players, he spotted a pretty blonde woman heading out the door.

"Hi, I'm Blake Geoffrion," he proclaimed as if she should already know, sticking out his hand and grinning.

Katelyn Deady didn't know, just as her future mother-in-law, Kelly Geoffrion, hadn't known who Boom Boom was when Danny had explained the family history on their first date. From his nickname, Kelly had assumed he was a boxer. Katelyn did know an ego when she saw one, though. The two exchanged numbers, but she didn't call, and Blake, after spending his teenage years toiling in monastic pursuit of sporting excellence, didn't really know how to ask her out.

~

On the ice, Blake sought the spotlight, wanting desperately to be *the guy*. Pounding his stick blade against the ice, calling for feeds, only to be caught in the wrong position when he got the puck. Yes, he could stickhandle and pass and shoot, but none of that mattered when he was caught out of position. Some of the other players whispered about his skating, still a bit ungainly even after the rigor of the NTDP. In all directions, he was being confronted with the harsh realities of a step up in class. He wasn't unfamiliar with unflattering comparisons—his family background made them inevitable. Danny had similar experiences when he advanced from the major juniors to the NHL back in Quebec. Blake heard the whispers (how could he not?), but they were drowned out by his own internal monologue, the voice of compulsive determination, which had driven him since his time at Culver. His body just refused to respond, weighed down by the classic rookie trap of trying too hard.

Eaves insisted that all his skaters recommit to defensive fundamentals. He would not allow anyone to be a defensive liability, even the flashy forwards who came to him basking in the brilliance of their own quick releases. Each and every one of his players had to learn a true two-way game, regardless of the name on the back of their jersey.

Blake's time on the ice was initially limited, his coach unbending in his demands. Blake's game was heavy on arrogance but light on offensive production. His coach was not surprised. "If you step back and take a look at the landscape of him as a hockey player, his pattern was one of not blowing you out of the water right away," said Eaves. Frustrated, embarrassed, Blake found his troubles and frustration only mounting as one bruising weekend series slammed into the next.

"I'm sure he thought he should be putting up better numbers," Eaves recalled. "But he had that stick-to-it-iveness, which was probably as big a part of his skill set as his ability to skate and play the game. Things did not always come easy, and I think he had that ability to persist and stay with it and eventually figure things out."

Canadian junior league boosters love to decry the thirty-four-game college season—about half the length of the juniors' schedule—and lack of fighting as not a self-respecting way to prepare for the NHL, a view perhaps colored by bitterness wrought from watching one prospect after another head south for campus life. Despite such naysaying, college hockey has risen in popularity as a pathway to the pros. The lighter schedule allows more time to focus on skills development and to refine the building blocks—passing, skating, shooting, set plays, face-offs, body positioning—that are crucial to separating great players from good ones. College hockey allows maturation at a slower pace, more directed coaching, and, for certain players, the chance to take a step back and connect the dots between brain and brawn.

All of this on-ice cultivation is complemented by an organic system of mentorship by upperclassmen, especially necessary for those fresh out of high school. Older players school the bigheaded, teaching them the ins and outs of campus life and leadership transition, their big-brotherliness infused with a healthy dose of school pride and a generous pinch of *you ain't the first to wear that sweater, and you ain't the last, and you sure as shit ain't the best.* Like any advice passed from one sibling to another, it often leaves a sour taste in the recipient's mouth.

At first, the older players "kind of hated us, and we hated them," said Blake. The freshmen who joined in the fall of 2006 thought the world of themselves, and the departure of a core group of players including Joe Pavelski, Adam Burish, and Robbie Earl from the preceding year's team—which had won the national championship—left the newcomers with a sense that they might just cruise right into the ice time they felt they so richly deserved.

The upperclassmen felt differently—and strongly. They took every opportunity to put the underclassmen in their place, eager to take the shine off the apple for the impertinent freshmen. They ribbed Blake far more often than they fed him the puck.

Blake, short on ice time and long on puck-shaped bruises, collected his first collegiate goal against Alaska-Anchorage on November 3, 2006. By mid-December, it stood out nakedly on the stat sheet as his sole tally.

His old roommate from USA Hockey, Patrick Kane, had taken the major juniors path instead of the college route, and as the World Juniors approached, the choice seemed to have been a sage one. Maybe Division I hockey wasn't everything it had been made out to be.

Ever since Team USA had won its first gold medal at the U20 World Junior Championships in 2004, the tournament had grown in importance both for the nation and for the young men chosen to fill out the roster. Winning it had been the realization of the vision USA Hockey had been pursuing since 1996. It had also sent expectations soaring.

Players selected to play for their country were allowed to leave their college or major juniors teams for several weeks to practice and prepare and then to play through the two-week tournament. The Wisconsin program had grown deeply intertwined with USA Hockey, and it had become an annual rite of passage for the very best Badgers players to be invited to suit up for their country, many for the second time. After six ugly weeks as a mediocre college player, a call from the roster makers for the December 2006 tournament was the last thing Blake expected.

But the call came from Ron Rolston, who had been named the US team's head coach for the World Juniors: "Yer gonna be on my shutdown line. I want you to bring that te-naa-city, block every shot for me. Can ya do that?"

Phone in hand, Blake stood stupidly and blurted out, "Are you serious?"

Over the first six weeks of the college hockey season, he had registered one goal. One goal! His once-promising college career was off to a disastrous start. Why did Rolston want him?

The USA Hockey team that would soon take the ice in Leksand and Mora, Sweden, had borrowed heavily from the college hockey ranks, and the roster was looking a lot like the U18 team from April 2006: Patrick Kane was back, along with Erik Johnson, Jamie McBain (now Blake's teammate at Wisconsin), Mike Carman, and Bill Sweatt. All except Kane were now playing in the WCHA. For three weeks, they would lay aside their new college uniforms—and the rivalries woven into the very fabric—and don the red, white, and blue.

For Blake, the break from the UW—from the practices, games, and roasting by his teammates—would be a welcome one. He would be back among his old NTDP buddies, comfortable in the warm embrace of USA Hockey.

After two weeks of practices, a twelve-hour flight to Stockholm, a three-plus-hour bus ride to Leksand, and just shy of six hours of hockey spread over eight days, Team USA was clinging to a 1–0 lead over Team Canada in the semifinals of the World Juniors, and Blake Geoffrion found himself thinking back to right before his departure from Madison. Davis Drewiske, the Badger captain, had pulled Blake aside and told him, "Don't talk so much. Listen more, relax. Quit trying to be the center of attention. Play for the team." Those words from the mouth of a fellow player finally penetrated where those of the coaches had been unable to reach.

Team USA's Rolston, watching his players hustle through a practice drill, could see that he had made the right choice. The Blake he saw battling in front of the net was the same coachable kid who had worn his country's colors the previous spring, not the obdurate college freshman from the fall. Something had changed. He was selfless and driven, even a little muted in his chatter. Drewiske's advice lingered, and Rolston, a witness to the change, promoted Blake to the third line, alongside his UW teammate Jack Skille.

The shutdown role Rolston had envisioned suited Blake, just as John Hynes had known it would two years before. It served his team well, all the way through the first round of the World Juniors and through the first two periods of the semifinal game against Canada. There was a newfound joy to Blake's game, a looseness that had been missing. And that made him even more furious when a whistle blew in his ear with less than ten minutes left in the third period and a one-goal lead.

Canada's Steve Downie was running around the ice chirping at everyone. Blake decided to run Downie across the rink and laid a clean check right through him. The linesman saw it differently and sent Blake off for a two-minute penalty.

Eighty-five seconds later, Blake banged the penalty box door open and stomped his way back onto the ice. Canada's Luc Bourdon had ripped a shot from the point over the shoulder of Team USA goalie Jeff Frazee, and Team Canada, with five thousand supporters cheering them on, had tied the game at one.

Future Montreal Canadiens star Carey Price turned away twelve shots for Team Canada in a ten-minute overtime, including one screamer off the stick of US blueliner Erik Johnson.

Now a shootout was going to decide who would advance to take on the Russians and vie for gold—"compelling drama," as the North American television announcers declared. Blake, still feeling like an impostor, tried to hide at the far end of the bench.

Coach Rolston pointed a finger at Kane. He'd be the first US American shooter.

Skating smoothly down the ice, side to side, his crossover step effortless, Kane moved right, then left, attempting to tuck the puck between cage and stick.

"Kane, stopped by Price!" exclaimed the announcer.

Canadian cowbells clanged their approval. The second Team Canada shooter snapped the puck low, glove side, to put his squad on the board; Team USA answered right back, slipping one by Price. Next up was Jonathan Toews, Team Canada's alternate captain, who skated up to the puck, rocked backward, dug his skates in, and then took off when the

referee blew his whistle. Toews danced up the ice with the puck, casu-
ally loaded his shot, and then sliced it past Frazee with ease.

Even the polite Canadian fans booed the next US skater, willing him
to miss, to stumble, but he took the puck, skated toward the net, and
whipped his shot stick side. The goal lamp flashed red. Frazee stopped
the next shot cold. All tied up at two goals apiece.

"And now Kane can win it for the United States. Patrick Kane, in on
Price, shoots, stopped by Price!" Or did he? Price snapped his legs shut on
Kane's five-hole bid, trapping the puck, but then Price then slid backward, right to the goal line. The US coaches yelled out, gesturing wildly,
and demanded a video review, insisting that Price had crossed the line.

Well versed in hockey gamesmanship, Team Canada's coach thrust
Toews back onto the ice before the referees could huddle. Toews's hur-
ried shot banged off the post and into the goal. The Manitoba native
had snatched the lead and stolen the momentum. Still crying foul, the
US coaches sent out Peter Mueller, who faked, shot, and scored. But
the relief was fleeting.

Round 6: Andrew Cogliano skated out for Canada, shot, and scored.
He leapt into the bench, where his mates hammered away at his back,
head, chest—whatever they could reach. But Jack Johnson answered
for the United States, aiming high up on the stick side and blasting the
puck past Price. On to Round 7.

Frazee faced off against Toews for the third time, who faked left and
then right, twitched his wrist, and sent the puck into the net, even
smoother, slicker, silkier than his first two attempts, if such a thing were
possible. Like Toews, Mueller had scored on his first two penalty shots,
and he was sent over the boards again; unlike Toews, Mueller missed
on his third. Team Canada would play for the gold. Or would it? As
the Canadians headed to the locker room to celebrate, USA Hockey's
Jim Johannson, fuming, yelled "Don't take your gear off!" at the US
players, demanding to anyone listening that Kane's second shot must
be reviewed. He was ignored. The IIHF later declared that the attempt
had been reviewed after the game and that there was no evidence that
the puck had crossed the goal line. Disgusted, the US team settled for

a bronze medal. Days later, the Canadians flew home with gold medals around their necks after defeating the Russian team in the finals. Hockey Canada has never forgotten that semifinal game; USA Hockey has never forgiven it.

Price, the Canadian goaltender, was named tournament MVP. At nineteen, he was a national icon. His team trailed only once during the tournament, in the third period of the semifinal game. He had kept the deficit to one goal, keeping his teammates within striking range in case a power-play opportunity presented itself. It did, and they had struck. And he answered the bell again in the shootout, turning away the final US shot to secure his team a berth in the championship game. Those two moments decided the entire tournament.

Blake watched both from a bench. It would be the last time, under his own power, that he was left just watching.

Blake Geoffrion loaded one twenty-five-pound plate and then another onto the barbell, then slid his body along the bench. He was a sophomore now, almost twenty, filling out nicely, and ready for the coming season, the last one having mercifully ended seven months earlier. The memories of goalless games and shootout defeats still drove him, but they didn't distract him. They focused him—on the next set, the next practice, the next run, the games yet to come. Bright lights blinked above, and around him stretched a spotless weight room, chest and triceps press machines, rows and rows of free weights, squat bars, squat stands, pull-up handles, battle ropes, bumper plates that kept plates from clinking together as scholarship athletes toiled diligently under the watchful eye of Jim Snider from the University of Wisconsin's Department of Strength and Conditioning. Remnants of last year's bigheaded freshman class dotted the room. There was Mike Davies, former North American Hockey League Rookie of the Year, and the long-legged John Mitchell, a homegrown product out of Wisconsin's Fox River Valley.

There were new faces, too. Important faces. Highly recruited faces. Canadian faces. Ever since the Bob Johnson days, Canadian players had been heading south for ice time, chasing girls and downing beers at whatever imitation of the Kollege Klub their campus could muster. Well, the good players, anyway. The truly great players, tracked since their bantam days by scouts and spectators, almost always stayed north. The combination of pressure to *Keep It Canadian*, a thousand times more intense than the judgment of a glowering Minnesota hockey commu- nity, was more than most young athletes could bear. For a US coach, getting a budding Canadian star to commit was the hockey equivalent of convincing a Cuban outfielder to defect.

But Mike Eaves had done it. Kyle Turris had been named Canadian Junior Player of the Year after tallying an astonishing 121 points as a seventeen-year-old, including a hat trick to win the Junior A National Championship. And in August, he would walk through the doors of the UW weight room, P1 visa stapled to his passport, clad in a new red tracksuit. The Phoenix Coyotes had drafted him third overall, banking in part on the strength and conditioning tutelage of the Wisconsin program: Turris was far from a lock. Some scouts had described him as "slight," a risky prospect in the rough-and-tumble ranks of the NHL. Or at least in the old NHL.

The 2004–5 lockout fundamentally reshaped the game of hockey, with lasting effects that would be felt at every level of the sport. After months of false promises and disingenuous offers, talks between the players union and NHL commissioner Gary Bettman imploded on February 10, 2005. No one suited up for the league that season, and months passed before the lockout ended. When it did, a new version of professional hockey emerged from the ashes. The effects of the league's rule changes soon trickled down to the college game, where the impact would be both instant and permanent.

Gone from the NHL was the center line; players were now allowed to make two-line passes, sending the puck from their own defensive zone all the way to the other blue line. Gone, too, was the dead space behind the net; goal lines were moved two feet closer to the boards, dramatically reducing the tendency for pucks to get stuck in the corners. Hockey had just been sped up dramatically, as if some omnipotent finger had pressed fast-forward.

Obstruction—hooking with the stick, holding, or other interference meant to stop opposing skaters from moving freely—would be penalized much more often. The old clutch-and-grab hockey just wasn't going to cut it anymore. Speed became an obsession, and size, well . . . if not an afterthought, it at least slipped a few rungs down the ladder. *Skating speed*, *hand speed*, and *shot speed* became the new buzzwords around the league.

Perhaps most important, the salary cap was here to stay. Bob Goodenow, the head of the players' union, had kept all seven hundred or so NHL players on the union side of the picket line for the better part of a year, warning them that if the owners got their way and a salary cap was implemented and linked to league revenue, it would lighten the players' pockets. Five days after the new deal was inked, a cap firmly in place to control costs for the owners, Goodenow resigned from his position. The billionaires had won yet again.

For all of the rules changes that rewarded speed, the new collective-bargaining agreement really rewarded frugality. Star talent still cost money, so overpaying the superstars meant that teams had to underpay other players. College players perfectly fit the bill. They were fast, and their entry-level contracts were cheap—the new collective-bargaining agreement had reduced the maximum salaries for rookies as well as opportunities for younger players to earn performance bonuses. Had the union sold out its incoming members? Maybe, but everyone loses in a negotiation. Some just lose more than others.

By filling a roster with teenagers prematurely plucked from the college ranks, teams could force third- and fourth-line veterans to take cheaper contracts, too. Cash-conscious general managers rubbed their hands with glee over the savings that bargain-basement youngsters represented. And for the college kids, subsisting on discount mozzarella sticks and sleeping on hand-me-down mattresses, even league-minimum contracts had more zeroes than most players had ever seen in one place.

The new NHL, obsessed with speed and thirsty for cost savings, seemed like a game tailormade for Kyle Turris.

Would it still have a place for the grandson of the man who invented the slap shot?

～

Wisconsin, Minnesota, Michigan, Denver, North Dakota, Boston College, Boston University. These had been the blue-blood aristocrats of college hockey, jockeying for the throne, for more than half a century. The occasional anomaly snuck in from time to time—Lake Superior State had won in '92 and again in '94, first beating Wisconsin and then Boston University, and Harvard had slipped by Minnesota in '89—but from 1948 to 2007, the Seven Kings of Campus had accounted for a total of forty-one championships. In eleven of the other years, one of those schools had been the first runner-up. Dominance had granted them the pick of the recruiting litter. *Tap, tap, tap* went the coaches' championship rings against the coffee tables in the suburban homes of Apple Valley, Winthrop, Bloomfield Hills, a cadence joined swiftly by the scratching of pens on commitment letters.

The coaching nobility bought their houses in campus towns, enrolled their kids in local prep schools, urged their wives to raise money for local Rotary Clubs and the Ronald McDonald Houses. *Come and stay, Coach. Win, be revered by every adoring fan and teammate and opponent who walks through the doors of our hallowed barn. Sleep well knowing that your teams will be made up of some of the best that North American hockey has to offer.*

Rule changes after the NHL lockout forced college hockey coaches to face their own reckoning. No longer could they rely on top-level players to stay for three or four years, maturing physically until they were ready to withstand the grinding and the fighting and the headhunting of the professional leagues. The best—or, rather, the precocious—would be gone in the blink of an eye, and their brief stays on campus would involve heightened scrutiny as development staff and dedicated media and bloggers obsessed over every muscle tremor and speculated wildly about readiness for an NHL roster slot and a Stanley Cup run. College hockey fans would suffer the most. As one former Badger hockey season ticket holder put it, "Every fan loses interest when you can't name the players."

A fundamental realignment was coming to the college game. Traditional powerhouse programs would soon risk falling into a state of perpetual prepubescence, unable to mature into national contenders. The most coveted recruits would become a liability, and schools that could adapt the way they recruited, coached, and played would win.

"We would talk about the fact that we couldn't get too many Kyle Turrises," recalled Eaves. "You were going to lose out in the long run."

Turris was a one-and-done the moment he signed his letter of commitment. The only question was whether he would finish out his freshman season or go pro right after the World Juniors in December.

The Badger hockey media showered Turris with acclaim. In a matter of weeks, he was being called Wisconsin's Golden Boy, and the press really couldn't be blamed for moving on from their infatuation with the scion of the Geoffrion family.

In his first year, Blake had hardly dazzled. He'd scored just two goals and assisted on four others, leading the team in only one category: penalty minutes. Heading into the 2007–8 college hockey season, he was going to have to battle for every minute of ice time. Rule changes or not, the NHL wasn't calling his number any time soon.

≈

In the Western Collegiate Hockey Association (WCHA), the toughest, nastiest division in college hockey, the University of North Dakota was the toughest and nastiest team of them all. No one ever thought to call the squad something clever—the Prairie Pugilists or some such thing. No such nickname was ever needed. All anyone ever said was "UND is coming to town." That was enough.

"They played hard. Their D would pinch all the time, they were aggressive to a fault. It was their style of play," said Davis Drewiske, the Badgers' team captain during the 2007–8 season. "If you could support the puck and get pucks behind their D, you could get the odd-man rushes."

On a Friday night three weeks into the season, the Badgers did just that. With five minutes left in the third period and the Badgers already up 2–0, Brendan Smith slid a pass to Josh Engel, who found Blake Geoffrion, who slammed the puck past Jean-Philippe Lamoureux. The Wisconsin crowd rained its signature *Sieve! Sieve! Sieve!* chant down on the hapless UND goaltender. Shane Connolly, the Badger goaltender, couldn't help but gloat with a tape recorder in his face after the game, smirking through a dusting of red beard, "I could see the puck. It looked like a beach ball out there tonight, and that's how I felt in the third period."

Kyle Turris wore a smirk, too, although his was shaded slightly by a pained grimace, still smarting after being walloped by six-foot-seven, 245-pound North Dakota defenseman Joe Finley.

Finley never took losses well. To be shut out by Wisconsin was an affront to his pride. The next night, in front of a packed Badger barn, was going to be different.

Finley and his teammates would see to that.

~

Bucky Badger, Wisconsin's athletics mascot, also stands six-foot-seven, with an enormous brown head that pokes out of a red-and-white-striped turtleneck sweater. On this occasion, his furry brown fingers sliced through the air in a derisive gesture, the object of his scorn scraping the ice for traction in the crease. Lamoureux's skates peeked out from beneath his white goalie pads.

The Saturday-night crowd of 15,237, twenty-four hours removed from a buoyant win, roared out its assessment of Lamoureux with each taunting gesture from their beloved mascot. *Sieve! Sieve! Sieve!* The fans knew their history: many had been in the same seats the year before, furious witnesses to an overtime defeat by UND on the night Wisconsin's national championship banner was raised to the rafters. Their anger still burned hot, and they wanted revenge for the disrespectful treatment of their program, past and present.

Only when the lights cut out and the familiar thundering notes of Metallica's "Enter Sandman" erupted from the speakers did the fans' collective loathing give way to adoration as expectant eyes pivoted to the home team's tunnel. One by one, the Badgers took to the Kohl Center ice, whipping themselves in a frenzied ring around the face-off circles. The whole scene conjured the atmosphere of a monster truck show, complete with hair-metal guitar chords, flashing strobe lights, and the piercing screams of female fans, but in moments it all gave way to the *swoosh* of skates on ice and the *thump* of pucks on sticks and the *huuurgh* of air being expelled from players' bodies, the clean and timeless sounds of a hockey game.

UND opened the scoring halfway through the first period, then made it 2–0 with three seconds left in the frame when T. J. Oshie poked a rebound past the Badger goalie. Oshie's chirping grated on the nerves of his opponents, but when Blake cross-checked Oshie as he celebrated his goal, it was no crime of passion. The hit was heavy but calculated, a proportionate response to the punishment UW's own smaller players were absorbing. Drewiske hurled his considerable bulk into the fracas as the period drew to a close, earning himself a double-minor penalty.

As the horn sounded to signal the start of the second period, the two Badgers sat shoulder to shoulder in the penalty box, chuckling over the dustup, pleased with their penalties, bumping fists in professional appreciation. As the ice shavings slowly melted off their skates, the sweat and the chill of the rink mixed together and ran down the blurred walls of the penalty box, which rattled with every hit. The pair didn't need to squint through the fogged glass to know what was happening.

Turris, their skill player, was getting rag-dolled around the ice by the North Dakota skaters. Finley repeatedly tackled Turris into the boards, and UND's Rylan Kaip entered every face-off with one objective: drive the freshman into the ice.

Those rat bastards, Blake thought, twisting the handle of his stick against his palms. He wasn't going to back down. He would use his instincts and physical dominance to carve out safe zones for the smaller players, savoring the contact of the corner dogfights.

"Hey, Blake, don't take any shit from those guys," offered a member of the rink staff as the penalty came to a close.

Blake nodded back at him. "You got it." He and Drewiske burst out of the box.

By the time the second period drew to a close, head coach Mike Eaves had seen enough. "Friggin' A guys, stick up for yourself and your boys out there," he snarled, the self-censorship at odds with the menace in his voice. With the second period winding down, the scoreboard read 3–0 North Dakota. Five more players—two Badgers and three Fighting Sioux skaters—had landed in the penalty box in the final minute of the period. Eaves had been here before. He knew that the loss was coming, just as he knew that his young team was likely to face the Fighting Sioux again, with higher stakes on the line, later in the season. They had an opportunity to grow as a group and to glue a little grit to their collective character along the way.

Whiskey-coated throats screamed from the stands into the void as the new period unfolded much like the last, escalating from chippy to nasty with each reckless hit.

The top line was out on the ice, Kyle Turris among them, with Turris's fellow first-round draft pick Brendan Smith anchoring the blue line. With four minutes to go and the Badgers down 3–1, North Dakota's Chay Genoway dumped it into the Badger zone. Smith scooped it up behind the net and was immediately pinned against the boards, the puck at his feet. He was jostled from behind as he tried to kick it free, his head down and neck extended, exposed, when Sioux captain Rylan Kaip raced along the rim of the rink and blindsided Smith. Turris, livid, ripped Kaip to the ice, and suddenly fists were flying as the rivals tore into each other, the stomping of thousands of spectators drowning out the sounds of sticks cracking against helmets.

Two more Badger players dived headlong into the action. On the bench, Blake watched as the donnybrook unfolded, standing shoulder to shoulder with his teammates, restrained by the assistant coach, yelling encouragement to his teammates, who were busy repaying the abuse they had endured all weekend. Even the coaches joined the fray, screaming obscenities at each other through the plexiglass barrier separating their benches.

Fans stood on their feet, rooting lustily at each punch thrown and head slammed into the unforgiving ice.

Finally the referees forced all ten skaters off the ice, huddled against the boards, and started assessing penalties—a total of more than 170 minutes.

The final horn blew. Wisconsin had lost.

No one was spared violence that night. As Joe Finley stomped down the runway off the ice, he brushed past Bucky Badger. Remembering the *Sieve!* chant that the oversized weasel had led earlier in the evening, Finley turned and slashed the critter across the shins. It was a fitting end to the weekend's circus.

As usual, Coach Eaves had been right. The raucous North Dakota series, a relic more typical of a bygone era, had cemented his young team's identity. What the Badgers lacked in elite goaltending or fourth-line depth, they more than made up with a simmering ardor that lent their hits just a little extra authority and made their shot blocking a little more incautious, their trash talk a little more personal. Their wins, when they came, were all the more gratifying.

They did not always beat the bad teams or win the close games, but they did enough to stay above .500 in the league standings—much to the chagrin of the Fighting Sioux. And for all the accolades bestowed on Kyle Turris, it was Blake Geoffrion who began to step up, game after game.

Wisconsin Badgers coach Mike Eaves speaks with
Blake during a game, 2009.

Photograph by Kelly Geoffrion, 2009.

Points racked up against Top 10 opponents seemed to be Blake's
forte: an assist against Michigan, a goal against Michigan State, another
goal and three assists against Colorado College, a pair of assists against
Denver. The Minnesota Golden Gophers were on the receiving end of
a pair of Geoffrion points, too—a goal and an assist. Blake's reinvigorated offense flowed from the quiet development championed by advo-
cates for the collegiate model. His skating had steadily improved, which
made him faster, allowing him an extra half second to pause, assess, act.
And increasingly to score.

Professional athletes, coaches, and scouts in many sports mutter incessantly about the game within the game, the details unseen by the
average fan, tiny elements shrouded behind the simple stats of goals,
assists, saves, runs, baskets and rebounds. They talk about "hockey sense"
with reverence—that uncanny knack for knowing where a puck or player
is going to be long before either gets there, for eating up ice time and

delivering clean checks and drawing penalties and edging an opponent ever so slightly off a puck just enough to give a shooter enough space to load the shot and then send it rifling off the goalie's pads and rebounding right back onto a linemate's stick blade for the easy tap-in.

Somewhere along the line, Blake had realized that natural skill and size, an impeccable pedigree, and even a boundless desire to win weren't enough. He had learned to study tape with the zeal of a fanatic, poring over it, predicting outcomes before the play had even begun. Coach Eaves watched, pleased, as Blake grew to love film study, becoming a compulsive analyzer of his own play and of any other hockey that happened to be flickering across a nearby screen.

Willingly or not, teammates were saddled with his obsession. "John, look at this, look at this," Blake would insist, dragging the six-foot-five Mitchell nearer to the screen, imploring that he internalize some fractional detail, just as Blake had done.

"Blake's one of those guys, when you're around him for a while, he can wear you out," recalled Eaves. "He can talk a dog off a meat wagon. But he made his teammates better with that enthusiasm."

The coach could not help but marvel at the growth of young Blake, so distant from the egotistical freshman who had struggled to score. Relentless about hockey. Not just playing it. Not just watching it. But stealing every ounce of understanding he could glean at every single opportunity.

College hockey had changed since the 1980s, with copious amounts of attention now lavished on and money now promised to the cream of the college crop. Turning a blind eye to booze-fueled pranking was a thing of the past. Still, the boys were beloved, with endless attention bestowed on them by team hangers-on and "another round on the house, fellas" frequently announced by the bartenders at the Kollege Klub. And there they'd be, shoulder to shoulder at the bar, beer bottles wrapped in twice-broken fingers, and Blake would be the guy using his free hand to gesture wildly at the TV screen and wax philosophical about the breakout speed on a play that hadn't even ended in a shot on goal.

By this time, Katelyn Deady was a bartender at the Kollege Klub, and she had left an impression on Blake that he couldn't shake. Sweet, kind, beautiful, the kind of woman he could bring home to meet his parents, a college sweetheart saddled with lovestruck clichés. *Attributes of a life partner*, now that he thought about it. At the first subtle hint from a mutual friend that his interest might be reciprocated, he rushed down to the KK, so desperate to strike up a conversation that he was willing to order one of the dive bar's cheeseburgers. The two began dating shortly thereafter. Katelyn was never dazzled by Blake's gradually snowballing celebrity status. Her interest in his hockey was polite and warm, her well wishes the same as if his passion had been stamp collecting or trout fishing. She was a grounding force and would remain so even as his star continued to rise.

As his sophomore season drew to a close, Blake trailed only Turris in points per game for the Badgers, with his ten goals and nineteen assists resulting in an average of a little under a point a game, an astounding leap forward from his freshman campaign made even more remarkable by the level of competition against which it had come. Four WCHA schools stood comfortably in the Top 10, and three more claimed Top 20 status. Many of his goals against conference opponents had been scored with two feet planted firmly in front of the net, battling defenders, screening goalies, and tipping pucks, much to the exasperation of his opponents.

Blake had taken the knowledge gained from Eaves and from highlight reels and applied it, one shift at a time, to his game. Injuries always bugged him, more than most. He *needed* to play, felt compelled to put his burgeoning hockey knowledge to good use. The newfound wisdom made its way from brain stem to fingertips, which were now whisking pucks past opposing goalies at a steady pace.

His never-ending chatter had won him all-hours access to the Kohl Center: Artie, the rink manager, was pleased to open up the facility for Blake any time. Blake regularly stopped by after class, the day's practice already under his belt, and laced up to shoot, shoot again, shoot endlessly, carefree and soaring with an entire rink to himself. More than anything, the self-imposed isolation, away from his teammates' banter, was a recognition of his own limits and of the necessity for more work than even the coaches demanded of him. The endless expanse of ice was a blank canvas, a challenge.

∽

The NCAA hired Jim Van Valkenburg as Director of Statistics in 1968, when statistical compilation was struggling to stand on wobbly adolescent legs. Van Valkenburg's role took on new importance when the NCAA basketball tournament expanded in 1975 to include at-large bids rather than solely conference champions. The lineup of teams invited to the tournament was no longer patently obvious, and new criteria had to be developed to evaluate the additional teams joining the Big Dance.

Van Valkenburg's rating percentage index (RPI) was rolled out in time for the 1980–81 season, receiving mostly scathing reviews from the sportswriters who had learned their craft—and based their salary-justifying résumés—on the hoary traditions of narrative and hunch. At the time of its implementation, each relevant statistic for the new calculation method, for every single Division I basketball game played across the country, was entered into the NCAA's computers *by hand*.

The RPI is calculated by weighted factors: 25 percent for a team's overall record, 21 percent for the record of a team's opponents, and 54 percent for the record of the opponent's opponents. Put simply, strength of schedule rules the day. Both wins and losses are weighted based on location, with road wins counting for more than home wins and road losses incurring less of a penalty than home losses.

College hockey's year-end tournament expanded from eight to twelve teams for the 1987–88 season, and by the early 1990s, the powers that be borrowed basketball's RPI and combined it with several other factors to compare teams and decide who should make the tournament. What had they used before? "A whole lot of cigar smoke," according to Adam Wodon, the longtime managing editor of *College Hockey News*.

The NCAA's hockey selection committee developed a computer program that ranked teams based on their RPI plus their record versus common opponents and their head-to-head records. The program, which debuted in the mid-1990s, yielded a single number—comparison wins.

US College Hockey Online, the original online-only college hockey media outlet, developed its own system, PairWise, that mimicked the NCAA's criteria and published the rankings throughout the season. The unfolding statistical wizardry entranced conspiracy-minded college hockey fans, who feverishly anticipated the NCAA tournament long before the last game of the season was played. When all was said and done, a computer in Indianapolis spat out a list of teams ranked by comparison wins, and the selection committee used those rankings to determine bids for teams that hadn't earned an automatic tournament slot by winning their conferences.

~

The college hockey players sitting around Davis Drewiske's apartment on Easter Sunday 2008 and surrounded by a growing pile of empty Keystone Light cans were oblivious to the machinations of the computer program analyzing their fate. Tonight, they were drinking with purpose.

Their regular season had ended more than a week earlier when they were swept out of the WCHA tournament by St. Cloud State, leaving the Badgers with a sub-.500 mark for the season. Any hope they had once cherished for a deep run to the Frozen Four had faded away.

Blake was sprawled on the couch, jostling for space with the big bodies of Drewiske, Kyle Klubertanz, Matthew Ford, and Josh Engel. ESPN played in the background. They were barely listening, joking with each other, chirping mercilessly as the school names were read out, many of them evoking foul-tasting memories of an almost-good season, until . . . *Wisconsin? Did he just fuckin' say Wisconsin? No. 16 seed—Are you kidding me?!*

The Badgers had snuck into the tournament thanks to the selection committee criteria, which included yet another obscure provision: teams under consideration.

Minnesota State–Mankato had beaten the Badgers twice, tied them once, and lost to them only once, but the Mavericks were out and Wisconsin was in. Why? Mankato, ranked fourteenth to the Badgers seventeenth, had earned more *total* comparison wins among *all* Division I teams. Comparison wins are matchups that never take place in the real world but instead are computer projections. However, the committee considered only comparison wins involving "teams under consideration"—that is, teams ranked in the Top 25, a quirk in the algorithm that benefited the Badgers.

Through a statistical contortion that no one, least of all the players, quite understood, Wisconsin was headed to the tourney, the lowest-seeded team in a sixteen-team tournament.

And those boys went absolutely ballistic, crowing to the skies at their good fortune. The puck would drop again for them this season, against Denver, the WCHA tournament champion, George Gwozdecky's team that always seemed to have their number. And the game would be played at the Kohl Center, where the Badgers had just led the NCAA in attendance for the tenth consecutive season. This called for a celebration. Drewiske and Co. marched off triumphantly to the Kollege Klub to accept the congratulations of the omnipresent puck heads.

While his teammates headed out to celebrate, Blake slipped off into the chilly night. Muscle memory was kicking in. Minutes later, he was whipping around the rink, clanging shots off posts and boards, stumbling and laughing to himself as sweat stinking of cheap beer poured off his nose. Back on the ice. Alone again.

A few team practices, a few classes, a couple beers (but not too many), the obligatory round of media interviews, and suddenly the week was over. Game night had arrived.

The Crease Creatures, the clamorous student supporters of Badger hockey, found their seats somewhat sheepishly; they, too, had been listening to the rumblings of discontent from the college hockey world about a team under .500 sneaking (stealing!) its way into the tournament, with the location just a little too convenient. So said the conspiracy minded.

"We had nothin' to lose," Blake recollected. "We played these guys a million times; we knew what we needed to do."

Sipping whiskey and Coke, the students, parents, working stiffs, and white-collar box-seaters watched as the first period unfolded and their team controlled the pace with supreme poise. The minutes ticked by, and the squad that had never seemed comfortable in its skin all year jelled before their eyes. Blake was at the heart of it all, winning face-offs, bullying Pioneers who happened to skate within his reach.

Nine minutes in, a puck squirted loose, and Blake chased it down, spinning, then whisked a pass to Jamie McBain, who fired a shot from the point. The rebound off the Denver goalie settled right at the feet of Mike Davies, who flicked it in to light the lamp and drag a skeptical hometown crowd headlong back into the spirit of playoff hockey.

Four Denver shots clanged off the posts, yet each heart-stopping report was suffocated by the singing and screams of the spectators, who could see their team skating loose, passing crisply, supremely comfortable. Four more Badgers tallied goals in the third period. Blake won four of seven face-offs and finished the evening with a plus-three rating. As the game ended and players fists bumped down the line, they broke into infectious smiles, eyes traveling up the Kohl Center aisles. Thousands of fans looked down beneficently, serenading their team with the alma mater anthem "Varsity."

One more win, one final push past an underestimating opponent was all it would take to make the Frozen Four. And UND was back in town.

≈

The same clanging of pucks of posts echoed through the Kohl Center the next evening, raw and hollow, sickening for a shooter and haunting for a goalie. Jean-Philippe Lamoureux, the Grand Forks native and North Dakota netminder who had been named a Hobey Baker semifinalist earlier in the year, felt each reverberation deep in his belly, the ugly sound a warning of how close his college hockey career was to its conclusion.

A Wisconsin defenseman had buried one early in the second, and UW's Cody Goloubef lucked into another late one in the period after his missed slap shot thumped against Lamoureux's posterior and flopped over the goal line, giving Wisconsin a 2–0 lead. Yet another Badger goal had been disallowed, and one more shot had rung off the post, its trajectory so convincing that the goal judge had mistakenly lit the lamp.

The Frozen Four was a period away, but the two-goal cushion didn't feel like enough. *The most dangerous lead in hockey.* Everyone knew the saying. No one said it out loud.

Wisconsin goalie Shane Connelly let one go through his legs to put UND on the board just over three and a half minutes into the third period; forty-seven seconds later, Ryan Duncan, the reigning Hobey Baker winner, scored the equalizer. The pendulum had swung, and when the buzzer sounded, overtime, ugly and unwelcome, had arrived.

North Dakota's Lamoureux had already blocked an incredible forty shots. Whispers of doubt began to return to Badger brains. *Did they belong here? Was the spotlight too bright?*

For Blake, the answers were *yes* and *never.* He had put in too many hours, in practice and out, not to feel ready. After ninety seconds of overtime hockey, Connelly clamped down on a puck, the play was blown dead, and Blake skated comfortably into the face-off circle, his broad back a wall between him and his goalie.

"Tur," he said, nodding at freshman forward Kyle Turris, "I got this one."

Turris shook his head. "I got it, I got it."

Turris skated in to take Blake's place in the circle, crouching across from UND's T. J. Oshie. Blake, poised a stick length away, watched what happened next in hideous freeze-frame. The referee dropped the puck, both skaters lunged forward, and Turris missed it. Oshie passed the puck to a teammate, who fired. When the shot rebounded, UND's Andrew Kozek sent it to the back of the net. Red light danced off the faces of the motionless Badger players, sickened at the sight of their antagonists embracing in celebration. North Dakota was headed to its fourth straight Frozen Four, and the Wisconsin boys were headed back to the couch, their season over. This time for real.

By the next morning, Turris had signed a professional contract with the Arizona Coyotes and was on a plane to Phoenix, while Drewiske inked a deal with the Los Angeles Kings. Before leaving Madison, however, the senior captain still had one piece of college hockey business to attend to.

The vote for team MVP was held that afternoon, and when the ballots were counted, Drewiske had won, the latest in a long line of Wisconsin alumni who exemplified the tradition they inherited. All Drewiske had ever wanted was to be a Badger. He was the undisputed team leader, a senior bound for the NHL, a homegrown product turned respected national champion. And his own MVP vote? Well, he had voted for Blake. Blake had the attitude, the work ethic. He was dependable and versatile, Drewiske thought, a constant competitor, "the guy you always wanted in your foxhole."

Along with Ben Street, Blake was officially elected captain for the 2008–9 season, his third with the program. Helped along by the hot hands of freshman forward Derek Stepan, who tallied nine goals and twenty-four assists, and the superb blue line play of Hobey Baker finalist Jamie McBain, second in points scored among all defensemen nationwide, the Badgers overcame a rocky start to make a strong case for another run deep into the 2009 NCAA tournament.

Blake had laid down another cornerstone campaign: fifteen goals (ten off the power play) and thirteen assists in the consistent style that teammates respect and coaches crave. He had put in countless hours at the rink long after his teammates had hit the showers, continuing his unwavering determination to outwork everyone else. He was nearly militaristic in his approach. Precise, commanding, battle-ready. Blake was relentless. Studying tape, dissecting body position and face-off crouches with his coaches, leaving no detail unexamined. He was forever being driven along by his own whispers, now that he had quieted his cocky chatter enough to hear them. *Your talent isn't enough. Your talent isn't enough.*

∼

The Badgers won twenty games that season, riding their superb team chemistry to a far better record than they'd posted during Blake's sophomore year. Nevertheless, March again found them on the bubble for NCAA tournament consideration, and RPI giveth and RPI taketh away. Minnesota, Ohio State, and Wisconsin had ended up tied at nine comparison wins, and Ohio State edged out UW by 0.002 on the RPI. For all their growth, Blake and his teammates were stuck watching the tournament from their couches. McBain, the WCHA Player of the Year, departed for the NHL shortly thereafter.

Would Blake do the same?

The Nashville Predators, who held his NHL rights, were not exerting any pressure. They liked what they saw, and he had a spot with the organization if he wanted one, but they were just as happy to see him spend his final year in the NCAA.

"I thought I was pretty ready to go," remembered Blake. "I looked hard at the roster, though, and said to myself, *What's one more year?*" The prospect of finishing his degree was appealing, too. Danny and Kelly had always stressed the need for education, telling their boys, "Get your degree. You're only as good as your last shift."

Blake wasn't the only veteran preparing to lace up again for Wisconsin. Brendan Smith had stuck around long after his fellow Canadian, Kyle Turris, had left, slowed in his development by injuries. Ryan McDonagh was going to be a junior after an eye-opening sophomore campaign. Ben Street, who had been a freshman on the 2006 national championship team, was rejoining the lineup following a year of recovery from an ugly knee injury. Blake was close with Adam Burish and some of the other leaders from the 2005–6 team, and he marveled at their camaraderie, the heroes' welcome they received when they returned to Madison, etched forever—together—in the Wisconsin hockey history books. "I wanted that."

The pressure to take up his family legacy, to restore the sequence broken by his father's status as an NHL bust, never dissipated, but professional hockey could wait. Blake had also been entrusted with Badger Bob's legacy.

$\sim$

The turnstiles of every college hockey arena sound different: some go click-click-click, an old-fashioned coffee grinder whirling steel against roasted beans; others groan and squeal and protest at the intrusion of yet another pair of hips wrapped in a thick winter coat, forcing them inward; still more clank rudely, pausing at their apex before plunging back into position. The fans, too, sound different; the long *ooh*s of Minnesota and the dropped *R*s of Boston, *dis* and *der* in Michigan's Upper Peninsula, *penalty bawxs* and *face-warshing* penalties in Bowling Green and South Bend. For some fans, the harsh edges of their homespun accents have been worn smooth after years of higher education and boardroom banter, while others sound raw, fresh from the factory floor, as blue-collar as a defenseman picking fights with the other team's enforcer. Students naturally get the most attention. They're young, vibrant, loud, and often liquored up. They scream and taunt yet look wholesome and photogenic enough for the big screen to capture their all-American expressions. Their apparel, fresh from the bookstore, comes marked with the clever name of their particular tribe. The Crease Creatures. Lawson's Lunatics. The Lynah Faithful. The Children of Yost.

And in a year or four, many will leave their college fandom behind, a warming remembrance of an undergraduate stay too fun to forget but too rowdy to continue. But others will stay—locals, young and old, who found in college hockey something missing from the pros, who are as much about the neighborhood or the city or the state as they are the university. They'll buy Blue Line Club lunches and bid on game-worn gear to benefit the Boys & Girls Club and take their kids to Skate with the Badgers or Wolverines or Spartans or Terriers and clamor for pucks to be tossed over the glass and then yammer excitedly over their shoulders into the back seat to try to paint a picture, never vivid enough, of weekend series long past. They will buy the newspaper just to complain about the recruiting coverage, tip back another Schlitz, and then plunge right back into the fundamental unfairness of the hockey-to-football ratio of attention on ESPN. Did anyone ask *these* fans what they thought of the NCAA being turned into a short-time incubator for the NHL? Did those great and grand hockey minds, who had transformed university programs from a destination into a way station, consider the potential impact on the already fraught life of college hockey fans when their most captivating, virtuosic, glory-granting players were ripped away *years before their time?*

Joe Meloni, a standard-bearer of the game at *College Hockey News*, has thought about this for years. "So much of sports fandom is based on tradition. You almost develop an innate responsibility to support the team. It becomes a part of people's personalities, how they identify. And fans want to feel that when the players are on the ice, they care about it as much as you do. Well, they do and they don't."

So many of the good players leave after three years. The really good ones now leave after two, and the great ones often make the leap before the ice has melted off their skates from the last game of their first and only season in town. In doing so, they rob the fans of the ability to get to know them, to develop affections and affinities and personal relationships, real or perceived, with the young men who wear the colors that mean so much more than just a student union and a humanities building surrounded by a collection of dorms. Many older fans never attended the college attached to their favorite hockey team yet love even more ferociously than the alumni. They desperately want to believe in the potential of every crop of young recruits, in the growth of the sophomores, the leadership of the juniors and seniors. They want names to be forever attached to numbers, for players to want to *earn* a place in the rafters. They give their love wholeheartedly. In return, all they want is loyalty, even on a finite timeline.

"Hey, look, drop your gloves. If you really wanna do this, drop your gloves. Let's get rid of the sticks," Mike Eaves barked as his two players. Blake wasn't thinking about the state of the game or his place in the rafters on that fall 2009 afternoon. He was furious at his teammate Ben Grotting for something—for unseriousness, for ignoring the coaches, for a stick knob up under the rib cage one too many times. *Drop the gloves?* Hey, if Eaves said so.

Blake and Grotting flung their mitts to the ice and grabbed each other's sweaters, cocked back their fists, and swung at each other, teammate status forgotten. They didn't care. Each wanted to bludgeon the face before him. For the past few weeks, the locker room had been a tense place to tape a stick. Brendan Smith and Mike Davies, two of the team's best players, had been healthy scratches to start the season, riding the pine while Wisconsin opened the schedule with a loss and a tie against Colorado College. The team possessed so much potential yet had already dug itself into a hole. Captain Blake had seen enough, and his teammate was in no mood for a lecture. Punches landed, heads rocked back, lips split, blood trickled, and the two tumbled to the ice, where hands immediately pulled them apart.

Eaves skated away, unconcerned. He was confident that the blood spilled would bring his players together.

"Blake was so competitive, we would race to the practice rink on our scooters in full gear and skates, and he would be pissed if he lost," remembered sophomore Derek Stepan. "Eaves squeezed every ounce out of his players. Some guys didn't respond well to it."

Blake did.

He had stepped up when pushed at Culver Military Academy and again when playing for Team USA. He wasn't afraid of a coach's bite, and he wasn't afraid to bite back. He drew strength from deep within and channeled it into a game complemented by born ability but in no way buoyed by it. The Geoffrion genes were a good hockey foundation, but they were not a guarantee of greatness, as his father's career had proven. If Blake was going to be exceptional, he would have to get there with a style all his own.

He had a compulsion for finding pucks in front of the cage, a one-timer from the slot that commanded respect and instilled fear, and a big mouth that ground down his opponents and enlivened his teammates. George Gwozdecky, the legendary coach of the University of Denver Pioneers, had checked the Badger roster before the start of the season and couldn't believe his eyes: *When is this guy going to turn pro?*

The Pioneers were on the docket for January 22 and 23, right in the meat of the season. Plenty of hockey stood between Eaves and his old teammate Gwozdecky. Minnesota, St. Cloud State, North Dakota . . . the giants of the WCHA loomed on the Wisconsin schedule. And even before those games, the Badger faithful would see a familiar name on the ice in the Kohl Center, this time on the back of a University of New Hampshire jersey: Blake Kessel, younger brother of Phil, who had daggered the Badgers back in 2006 and then danced gleefully in front of an irate Kohl Center crowd, was off to a scorching start—three goals, seven assists, and a plus-four rating just four games into the season.

Everyone in a Badger sweater knew what it meant to have a Kessel back in town. Three of Blake's future teammates, including his eventual roommate and linemate, Mike Davies, had been in the stands that night on a recruiting trip, and as Davies recalled, "I've never heard an arena boo that loud. Ever." Blake had heard the story not only from them but also from former UW captain Adam Burish. Each touch of the puck by a Kessel was an affront to any self-respecting, grudge-holding Badger.

When the ice chips settled from the weekend, twelve goals had been scored, ten of them by Wisconsin. With bloodied bodies and bruised egos, the Wildcats boarded a plane back to Durham, and the Badgers saddled up for a triumphant night of celebration, their own bruises forgotten.

Blake had been held without a point . . . but so had Kessel. "Blake made it a personal mission to be a pain in his ass the entire weekend," the *Wisconsin State Journal*'s Andy Baggot recollected. "Hit him, chirped him, laid down good, clean hits. He felt it necessary to send a message and shut down their best player every minute." Bird-dogging Kessel hadn't won Blake Player of the Week honors or a coveted spot on ESPN's nightly Top 10. It had, however, helped his team bank two more wins, weighty numbers that were already whirring within the RPI machine.

~

Skaters around the conference—hell, around the country—knew that the penalty box at Ralph Englestad Arena was a place you wanted to avoid. It wasn't just that the North Dakota fans were mean. They were, yes, but they were also damn clever, obsessed with hockey, fiercely proud of their team's enduring success, and, to hear them tell it, personally responsible for reducing any college student who laced up in the visitors' locker room to a distracted, distraught, jellylike mass of nerves.

Ryan McDonagh, now in his third season at Wisconsin and an anchor on the blue line, was determined to stay out of the penalty box. UND was too good—ranked third in the country—and fans at the Ralph were already drooling in anticipation of the visitors. McDonagh's resolve lasted for all of fifty seconds: a North Dakota player caught the defenseman in the mouth with a stick and received a fist to the head in return. So now here he was, the hard plastic of the bench under his breezers, the needling of the Sioux supporters burrowing in his ears. Invoking his mother's name, they jeered, "Hey Ryan, does Patricia know you're in here?" He just shook his head and grinned. They were good; he had to give them that.

The teams ground through the next two minutes of four-on-four, the pressure building. Back at even strength, the Badgers began to reclaim neutral ice, sending clean passes *whup whup* into the offensive zone. Late in the period, on came Wisconsin with the puck, which landed with a zip on Blake's stick tape; Blake fed it to Craig Smith, who scored, just like they had planned.

As the period dwindled to a close, Smith returned the favor, finding Blake, feet spread wide and arms cocked back, and the puck careened past goalie Brad Eidsness for a 2–0 lead. The two teams skirmished in the latest violent outburst of a decades-long conflict, finesse forgotten.

For the final forty minutes of the game, the Fighting Sioux lived up to their moniker, shoving, tripping, and clutching the Badger players. The penalties mounted: roughing, cross-checking to the head, unsportsmanlike conduct, a check from behind that got UND winger Brett Hextall tossed. Wisconsin received its share of penalties too, and late in the second period, with a Badger in the penalty box for tripping, UND scored its first goal. And with Ryan McDonagh back in the sin bin during the third, North Dakota scored another power-play goal to knot the game. Badger and Sioux players traded penalties for the final ten minutes, with a late Wisconsin infraction sending the visitors into overtime down a skater. Tight checking and efficient execution by Blake and the rest of the penalty-kill unit allowed the Badgers to escape with a tie.

Furious with themselves for taking the bait, the UW players marched back to the visitors' locker room, stewing. When a bathroom stall door was ripped off its hinges, no one said anything. Coach Eaves launched into a predictable tongue lashing, but Blake, grounded and optimistic, and his nonstop chatter soothed the tempers of those sitting around him. His loquacity, once a liability, was being put to good use just as the season seemed to be hanging by a thread.

The Sioux succumbed to the Badgers' forechecking onslaught the next night, dropping the second game 4–3. Blake drew first blood for the Badgers in the opening frame, and Brendan Smith scored the game winner with a nifty wrister late in the third period. Blake had entered the series as the Badgers' scoring leader and left with two more goals and an assist. More important, however, the completeness of his play had earned the begrudging respect of the UND players, coaches, fans, and press.

Brad Elliott Schlossman, the ubiquitous reporter for the *Grand Forks Herald*, lingered in the UND locker room after the Saturday game, listening to the chatter of names repeated with reluctant admiration, including those of future NHL blueliners Ryan McDonagh, Brendan Smith, Jake Gardiner, Cody Goloubef, and Justin Schultz. But, according to Schlossman, on a "really good . . . team with a lot of guys, Blake is *the* guy. He is that special, *the* difference maker, the guy that scored the big goals and just, oh, yeah, he is good."

That weekend series was the beginning of Blake Geoffrion's Hobey Baker campaign. He had grown first into a dependable producer and from there into an elite, protean player. Across the nation, coaches were sitting at their desks that Monday morning, opening emails, watching clips, and reading recaps from the weekend's games.

Among those coaches was Minnesota State–Mankato's Troy Jutting. What he saw, through clouds of omnipresent cigarette smoke, riveted him. Here was a true two-way player, a guy who played heavy in the face-offs and in the corners, who scored at a terrifying pace, who simultaneously embodied the roles of leader, enforcer, scorer, and penalty killer. Blake had really come far, hadn't he?

Brendan Smith had also showcased his elite hockey skills in Grand Forks, and the Wisconsin athletic department had gone into overdrive to package highlights for the viewing pleasure of Hobey voters. The players might have responded to questions about the award with modesty and shrugged shoulders, but the most obsessive observers, whether coaches, announcers, fans, or former players, could talk about little else.

Halfway through his senior year, Blake had taken on a new role. To the standard burden of a star student-athlete—the morning practices and weight room sessions that left him yawning in class, the afternoon practices and evening study time with tutors, date nights with Katelyn, film study, beers with the boys at the Kollege Klub, injury rehab—and his late-night solo practices, he added the duties of an assistant coach. He doled out discipline or encouragement as the situation demanded and kept tabs on his teammates' pizza consumption, girlfriends, family illnesses back home. Every other Monday, he would sit down for lunch with Coach Eaves at the venerable Nitty Gritty bar and grill on North Frances Street, and the two would pore over line charts, their conversation drifting seamlessly from power-play units to academic performance and back again.

"Coach," Blake broke into Eaves's diatribe about the previous weekend's opponents one Monday, "I've got something you're not gonna want to hear." Blake paused and took a breath, noticing the twitch pulsing along Eaves's clenched jaw.

Blake had prepared a speech about his coach's in-game reaction to bad plays. Some UW player would make a mistake—lunge for a puck and give up a scoring chance or whatever—and Eaves would drop to his knees behind the bench and scream *Fuck!* into a clenched fist. The whole team would seize up, the freshmen especially, clutching at their sticks for some kind of reassurance. Tense and jumpy, they would make more mistakes, and the cycle of reaction and re-reaction would repeat itself.

Eaves's spoon clattered into his bowl, soup sloshing over the sides. His face was rigid.

"You don't know what the hell you're talking about," he snarled. "Don't you ever tell me how to coach my team."

He stood abruptly, the legs of his chair scraping against the wooden floor, turned, and walked out, leaving his captain to pay the check.

At 6:30 the next morning, Eaves called Blake, demanding that he be sitting in the coach's office in thirty minutes. When Blake arrived, Eaves gestured him into a seat. For a moment, the two stared at each other, unspeaking.

"I was up thinking about what you said all night," confessed Eaves. "You're right. I'll change it."

$\sim$

Blake could not seem to go a weekend without notching a goal. He had potted the lone tally in the series opener against St. Cloud State and scored again the next Friday against Michigan State (assisted by Brendan Smith) and Saturday versus Michigan (with Smith again providing an assist along with a goal of his own). Then back at the Kohl

Center, Blake recorded his first hat trick (two more Smith assists), earning a text from Danny back in Tennessee: "It's about time."

By Christmas, Blake had twelve goals and four assists; Smith had five
goals and fourteen assists. Their half-wall guy on the power play, Derek
Stepan, was also collecting points at a steady clip, and to the west and
east, Rhett Rakshani in Denver and Gustav Nyquist at the University of
Maine were making their own strong cases for the Hobey Baker Award.

The Badger boys would have to wait until the NCAA tournament
to have a shot at Nyquist and the Black Bears, but the Denver series, to
be played in Madison under the waving fingers of the Crease Creatures,
was only three weeks away. The *Denver Post* had already declared Denver
goalie Marc Cheverie the presumptive Hobey Baker front-runner, only
slightly ahead of Rakshani in the hometown rankings. According to the
Post, Wisconsin's Geoffrion would be lucky to crack the top 10.

Denver at the Kohl turned out to be Blake's magnum opus. Pioneers
head coach George Gwozdecky tried to warn his players: "This guy can
hurt you in so many ways. Pay attention to him!"

Gwozdecky was coaching the No. 1 ranked team in the country, with
two Hobey Baker contenders, and Denver had won seven of the last eight
matchups in Madison. No matter. He knew a war was coming. Better
than most, he understood what a player like Blake Geoffrion meant to
a college hockey team.

Denver started Friday night with a 1–0 lead on a shot from Joe Col-
borne and added a second tally less than two minutes into the third
period. Just as the game seemed to be creeping out of reach, Blake,
standing tall in front of the net during a power play, tipped the puck
into the net to bring his team—and the crowd—roaring back into the
game.

Mike Davies slid another past the Denver goalie, and Blake netted his
second of the night on a beautiful feed from sophomore Jordy Murray
with 11:17 left in the third. Thousands of fans danced and yowled—and
of course chanted *Sieve!* at Cheverie.

The Badgers then killed three consecutive penalties in the final ten minutes of the period. Its shutdown unit, led by Blake and John Ramage, collected bruises and blocked pucks without flinching. Finally, with both teams at full strength, the two skated gasping to the bench for a brief respite.

The Pioneers scored twenty seconds later to knot the game with less than two minutes to play, and after a scoreless overtime, players and fans alike walked out of the arena with a distinct feeling of unfinished business. A tie, a sister-kisser after such a beautiful comeback? Unacceptable.

~

More than fifteen thousand fans turned out for the rematch the following night and were treated to a spectacle reminiscent of the run-and-gun days of the 1980s.

The game featured twelve penalties and seven goals, among them a real wall-hanger of a wraparound from Jordy Murray that had started with a feed from Blake and a Michael Davies tip-in off a Justin Schultz wrist shot in the third that put the Badgers ahead for good. It was undoubtedly the series of the season.

With the college hockey world watching, the Badgers had beaten the best.

~

The team was already being compared to the 2006 national champions, a slippery slope of ego-inflating chatter for impressionable young players. As the magical moments continued to pile up—a win against Michigan, outdoors at Camp Randall Stadium, with fifty-five thousand in attendance, a 7–4 victory over St. Cloud State on Senior Night, a road sweep in Mankato, a road win against Minnesota to take the season series lead—the risk of bigheadedness grew right alongside.

Eaves understood the narrow window for success and the fragility of any season in the one-and-done era. He and Blake talked about the situation endlessly, probing strength, anticipating mental lapses, Blake defending his players and their proven work ethic even as Eaves insisted on another run, another lift, special power-play practices before the regularly scheduled ones. On the ice, Blake shouldered responsibility for his teammates' effort. He cheered their hustle and he chastised their sloth. "When I saw guys slacking, humping the dog, I was in their face," said Blake. "I was the one that drove, because it was on me. I didn't want to break that trust with Eaves—ever." Both he and his coach felt the weight of their impending tournament run, particularly after failing to earn a bid the previous year.

∾

Mike Eaves had become something of a hockey philosopher since he had moved from the ice to behind the bench. He read voraciously, his desk piled with leadership books and inspirational quotes written on scraps of paper mixed in with miniature whiteboards still bearing *X*s and arrows outlining power-play schemes. He was always searching for new ways to inspire, to cut through the wear of a long season. Among those piled papers was a recounting of a Socratic parable to which Eaves kept returning:

> A proud young man came to Socrates asking for wisdom. Socrates, recognizing a pompous fool when he saw one, led him down to the sea, put his strong hands on the man's shoulders, and pushed him under. Thirty seconds later Socrates let him up.
> "What do you want?" he asked again.
> "Wisdom," the young man sputtered, "Oh great and wise Socrates."
> Socrates pushed him under again. Thirty seconds, thirty-five, forty—then Socrates let him up. The man was gasping.
> "What do you want?"
> "Air!" the young man yelled. "I need air!"
> "When you want wisdom as much as you have just wanted air," Socrates intoned, "then you will begin to find wisdom."

Eaves read the story over and over, memorizing each line, envisioning every detail. He had been waiting for the right moment to use it.

Sitting in the Badger locker room, Blake's latest joke was cut short by the voice of his head coach.

"Get your games goin' tonight. You need to be prepared for them!" barked Eaves.

This for Alaska-Anchorage, the perennial cellar dwellers of the conference? With a No. 3 ranking in the national polls and an all-but-assured top seed locked up for the NCAA tournament, the Badgers' mood was loose, with wadded balls of stick tape tossed back and forth around the dressing room. Who was going to call the girls to meet them after the game?

The opening series of the WCHA tournament would be a tune-up, a gentle dipping of toes in the water before the gauntlet of the conference playoffs, the NCAA tournament, the Frozen Four, the national championship. Distracted players rolled their eyes as Eaves insisted they follow him into the showers.

In the center of the tiled floor was a folding chair on which sat a cooler filled with water. Eaves walked behind the chair and faced his team.

"Little, come over here. Can you hold your breath for fifteen seconds?"

Freshman Ryan Little replied that he could and, after another glance at his coach, thrust his entire head beneath the surface of the water, Eaves's hand on the back of his neck.

Fifteen seconds dragged by, and when Little moved to raise his submerged head, Eaves held him in in place. Little flailed wildly, his struggles slopping water over the sides of the cooler, the iron grip of his coach keeping his head immobile. Frantic, Mike Davies kicked the folding chair, sending the cooler flying. Eaves released his grip and Little sprung upward, gasping and spluttering.

"You see how he was fighting for his life? That's the way they're going to be fighting for their lives against you tonight! When you want to win as bad as Ryan wants to breathe, then we'll have something."

Without another word, Eaves marched out of the showers, his players parting silently to let him pass.

Little, still dripping with water, turned to hide an impish grin. The whole episode had been a setup, a literal demonstration of a metaphoric teaching. Eaves and Little had planned it in advance. No one else had a clue.

"We didn't have an ocean in Wisconsin," Eaves later reflected, "so I used a cooler in a locker room."

The Badgers won that night, 4–1.

Four weeks later, they were playing in the national title game.

The Boston College Eagles were facing off against the Wisconsin Badgers for the 2010 NCAA hockey national championship. So, what did that mean? It meant that in the semifinals, the Badgers had trounced an overmatched Rochester Institute of Technology squad, 8–1, while Boston College had hammered home seven to cruise past Miami University. Fourteen days earlier, the Badgers had won the West Regional, defeating St. Cloud State in the final after Blake Geoffrion had ripped a shot hard from the high slot to give his team a lead it would not relinquish against the Vermont Catamounts in the semis.

It meant that two of hockey's preeminent programs were squaring off on the sport's biggest stage, Wisconsin chasing its seventh national championship, Boston College its fourth, in a rematch of the 2006 title game. The best two defensive corps in the nation would be blocking shots and finishing checks and bullying forwards and goalies in a blueline battle that had old school puckheads salivating; Carl Sneep and Brian Dumoulin and Philip Samuelsson for the Eagles, Brendan Smith and Ryan McDonagh and Jake Gardiner and Justin Schultz for the Badgers. Midwest versus Northeast, Mike Eaves versus Jerry York.

As is usual at the Frozen Four, the Hobey Baker Award ceremony had taken place the night before the final. For the first time, however, a player from the storied University of Wisconsin hockey program had raised the trophy.

Blake had edged out Maine's Gustav Nyquist, the nation's leading point scorer, and New Hampshire's Bobby Butler, who led the country in goals, to achieve a feat that had eluded all the Badger greats who had preceded him—Chelios, Elliott, Suter, Richter, Heatley. The thirty-member selection committee, composed of a coach and an official from each of the six conferences, a half dozen college-focused NHL scouts, and select members of the media, had seen the unparalleled completeness of Blake's game. He was compared to the quietly brilliant Tomas Holmström, the "screening machine" who had exasperated opposing goalies for the Detroit Red Wings throughout the '90s. Fear of a Blake-tipped puck left defenders second-guessing themselves, spinning in circles. It also left goalies dejected and opposing coaches jealous.

Blake looked the part, too, the consummate cawlidge hawkey player, all shaggy hair and muscles. Tall and broad-shouldered, he wore a dark suit and a smile that peeked out from beneath his dorm room excuse for a mustache. The all-American All-American, a hockey dynasty realized in the flesh, casting a shadow over the statue of Hobey Baker. He had been named the best player in college hockey that season, and everyone in the audience understood why.

The lofty offensive statistics—twenty-eight goals and twenty-two assists—told only a fraction of the story. Only by watching every game could Blake's skill, generalship, and overall grittiness be appreciated. His was the tale of a player who could have been unremarkable, another big-bodied player's son who just never quite lived up to the pedigree of his forefathers. Instead, he had embraced the *C* emblazoned on his chest, the legacy of the colors he wore and the history he had inherited—his family's and his team's. He had molded himself into an exceptional machine of consistency and production, the ultimate coach's player. In doing so, he had carved out his own spot in hockey history.

"When the One Great Scorer comes to mark against your name, he writes—not that you won or lost—but how you played the Game." Grantland Rice's famous quote flashed across the screen as the story of Hobey Baker played before the assembled fans, coaches, players, and their families.

Bob Lindauer, perhaps the most faithful of the Wisconsin hockey faithful, was watching the ceremony from the audience. He exploded

Blake takes media questions after receiving the
Hobey Baker Award for the 2009–10 season.

Photograph by Joe Koshollek, 2010.

to his feet when Blake's name came blasting through the loudspeakers, clapping and stomping with pride. His memory was impeccable—he could recall when college players lived with billet families and Shagnasty's served cold beer and warming whiskey right across the street from the Dane County Coliseum. Lindauer had loved Badger hockey unconditionally for a quarter century, just as his counterparts in Boston and Minneapolis had loved the Terriers and the Gophers. Even if the game he so loved felt like it was slipping away.

He had loved despite the decline of the Blue Line Club and the rise of the one-and-done. Despite the fact that college hockey was being picked clean of its talent by the NHL, which promised players riches and playing time that sometimes materialized and sometimes didn't. Lindauer bemoaned—but didn't resent—the rising ticket prices that kept working-class families from attending games. He missed the days when players were familiar faces around the community, signing pucks at charity events and shoveling driveways for the old folks, but nostalgia didn't stop him from sharing the tickets bestowed on him by the UW athletic department as a thank you for all his years of fandom, passing them out to families with young kids and evangelizing hockey in the Bob Johnson tradition. He watched the pro scouts gain more and more access to the locker room and wished them well, though he also wished that the same open-door policy applied to grade-school kids and old-timers. He couldn't foresee the conference realignment that was coming, bringing to an end the old WCHA and its mighty rivalries as the powers that be sought more lucrative arrangements at the expense of longtime fans.

On that April night in Detroit, if someone had reminded Lindauer of how college hockey had changed, of all that it had lost, he would not have cared. A Wisconsin Badger had been declared the country's best college hockey player. He had stayed in Madison for four years and had brought his team to the doorstep of a seventh national championship. Lindauer watched the young man he had moved into the freshman dorms lift the Hobey Baker Award high into the air, clapping like a proud uncle and thinking that if Badger hockey had a Mount Rushmore, Blake had just earned his place on the mountain.

As the crowd milled around Blake, his beaming parents nearby, the congratulations of the hockey community bubbled through the room. An American player had won the award, the senior captain of a blue-blood program, at a time when senior captains were becoming the exception and senior captain superstars a species nearing extinction. A new chapter had been added to the Geoffrion/Morenz family history, adding an American great to the Canadian pedigree.

"Blake truly seemed to love being *the guy* for that program. He had an intense love for the University of Wisconsin and its fans, and he had become a talisman of the program," recounted Joe Meloni. The old guard of college hockey, the brain trust, which had fiercely, jealously guarded the institution from a slide into just another major junior league, was tickled pink by the magic of the moment.

Ever the single-minded team leader, Blake answered all inquiries about his personal legacy with polite deferrals: "My ultimate goal, and I've said this over and over, is to win a national championship. I want to do it for my team."

∽

Like Wisconsin, Boston College was experienced and deep. Some on the squad, including goaltender John Muse, had played on the 2008 national championship team. The Eagles protected leads with a ruthless ferocity, a hallmark of the Jerry York era. Every fall, York and assistant coaches Mike Cavanaugh and Greg Brown reconstructed a cold-blooded puck-control machine. *Force a turnover, dump the puck off, change the line.* Do it again and again and again until the horn sounded. The system had taken the Eagles to four title games in five years.

They were fast up front, too, and Cam Atkinson, arguably the best winger in the country, was the fastest of the lot. In contrast to the WCHA gore that Wisconsin had faced during the season, the final game wasn't going to be a slugfest. It would be calculated and deliberate, with moves mapped out three plays in advance and countermoves countering countermoves in clever fashion from end to end. More than thirty-seven thousand fans would be watching the opening face-off from the bleachers of Ford Field, a temporary rink plunked on the football field, the postures and pores of Geoffrion and Atkinson and all the rest projected in gargantuan detail on the Jumbotron. Sixty minutes of hockey left in the season. There was no room for error.

∾

"The power play still underway from the Eagles, that's gonna be bounced off the near side boards, Whitney, chance, shot, scores!" declared ESPN's Gary Thorne. And just like that, 12:57 into the first, York had his lead. The Wisconsin-heavy crowd groaned in disappointment. This was bad. This was very bad. Ordinarily, one goal was nothing. Tonight, it felt like everything.

Muse went mostly unchallenged over the first twenty minutes as the Badgers managed only five shots on goal. Wisconsin squandered a power play with only one weak chance early in the period, never finding a rhythm as Eagle defenders shut down shooting lanes and blocked shots. Davies sent a puck wide to the right of the goal, and then Blake, at home on the edge of the crease, had the door slammed in his face with a clean save by Muse.

"After being in the coaching business for twenty-five years, you can have really good players, good coaches, strategy, and health, but there's an *X* factor that is out of your control," said Eaves. "You could just say that's being fatalistic."

Eaves knew the adjustments that needed to be made. Limit turnovers, control the puck for longer stretches. Still, he could already feel something slipping away.

"It was the first test on us of having to be really patient," Ryan McDonagh said of the game at that point. "We can't start pressing and getting away from everything that had made us successful."

Midway through the second period, the temporary ice sheet perched atop the Detroit Lions' home turf began to disintegrate. This wasn't a good sign. At the next stoppage of play, the referees called out facility staff to reconstruct the ice. Despite the TV cameras, the throngs of spectators, and the hoopla, it started to feel like the last game of hockey before the lake thawed in the spring, with players skating through slush.

And then with 5:46 left in the period, Badger fans rose from their seats as if pulled upward by ten thousand puppet strings, watching as Davies received a perfect pass from Gardiner and loaded up the puck for a wrister into the net left suddenly exposed by the Boston College goaltender—a shot he had made ten thousand times in practices and in games. But as Davies went to send it, the puck leapt off the fractured ice and he whiffed completely. Wisconsin fans could manage no more than a whimper. Still 1–0.

~

Mike Eaves delivered a scorching speech during the second intermission, stomping, pointing, blowtorching his players. Even the upperclassmen, veterans of dozens of fiery pep talks, felt a renewed surge of fortitude.

His words had lit a fire; ninety-eight seconds later, the Eagles had reduced it to embers. Atkinson gathered in the short pass from Joe Whitney, blew past Justin Schultz, and drilled a backhander past Scott Gudmandson to make the score 2–0. Less than two minutes later, freshman winger Chris Kreider redirected a pass to increase BC's lead. As the Eagles hugged and spun with joy, Badger sophomore Derek Stepan lay concussed and motionless against the dasher boards. His teammates helped him off the ice, their shoulders sagging as they watched him stumble back through the tunnel and into the locker room.

Atkinson went five-hole on the power play minutes later to add another, and Matt Price clanged a fifth goal into the back of an empty net to bring the hideous spectacle to a close.

"For Boston, for Boston, we sing our proud refrain . . . for Boston, for Boston, till the echoes ring again!" The brass band blasted out the notes, John Muse disappeared under a mass of teammates, and the cameras swung to capture the elation on the faces of York and his coaching staff.

At the other end of the ice, the Badgers stood limply, faces blank. For most, including Blake, it was the last time they would ever don the cardinal red and white.

~

"How do you mourn an opportunity lost forever?" asked Andy Baggot in the next morning's *Wisconsin State Journal*. Well, if you were the Badgers, you did it together, at the Kollege Klub. Katelyn was tending bar there, and she felt sad for them all but especially for her boyfriend, who would never get to play with this group of buddies again.

She poured a round, filling the glasses to the brim with the KK's newest shot: the Hobey Blaker.

Blake Geoffrion had finally earned a nickname.

chapter 5

THE PROS,
AND THE END

Blake Geoffrion's professional career should have begun with a burst burst of glory. The fourth generation of his family to earn his living playing hockey at the highest level the sport had to offer—a first for the league. The first player from Tennessee to enter the NHL, drafted by his hometown team. A rookie contract signing, planned by a gleeful Predators' PR department, to be held at Granbery Elementary in Brentwood. A homemade sign proclaiming "Welcome back, Blake!" hung in a classroom where he had once learned to scrawl his name in block letters, and four of his former teachers stood off to the side, smiling from ear to ear. None of them had ever been to a hockey game, but they had all pitched in to buy a Predators' season ticket package. The stuff of young boys' dreams, lived out on countless frozen ponds and driveways, come to life.

Days after returning to Madison with the Hobey Baker trophy in tow, Blake headed down I-94 to join the playoff-bound Milwaukee Admirals, Nashville's minor league affiliate in the professional American Hockey League (AHL). He rang up two goals in his second pro appearance and was named Hero of the Game, a 6–0 trouncing of the Chicago Wolves that positioned his new team to beat its top-seeded opponent and began yet another deep playoff run. That first pro goal had been a gem, a slick wrister launched between face-off circles, so pretty that even Blake had to stop to admire it.

And then an unlucky crash into the boards the next night broke the spell. A footrace with Nathan Oystrick into the corner of the Bradley Center rink left Blake kneeling in pain on the ice with a wrenched ankle and a twisted knee that would require months of rehab. His first professional season was over. There would be no glorious call-up to the Big Show in Nashville, no matchup against his old USA Hockey team-mate, Patrick Kane, in the Western Conference quarterfinals when the Predators took on the Chicago Blackhawks.

David Poile had joined the Nashville Predators as the team's inaugural general manager in 1997 and had watched thousands of players over his career, becoming the winningest GM in the history of the NHL. He knew the timeless value of a two-hundred-foot center as well as anyone and described Blake as "an ideal pick for us. Even if he always took a bit of time to get his feet wet."

As far as Blake was concerned, his feet were plenty wet. For all the pomp and circumstance of his contract signing and the puff pieces in the Tennessee sports pages about his hockey lineage, time was ticking.

～

The summer of 2010 had come and gone, and Blake had spent most of it rehabbing his ankle in Chicago, where Katelyn had moved after graduation. He got healthy but wasn't the rink rat that he'd been in college or the gym rat he'd been during summers past. It was almost as if some of that old freshman cockiness had crept back into his head. Then came autumn, and with it Predators' training camp. Blake didn't make the big club and was assigned to Milwaukee for a little more development. As Poile had predicted, Blake needed some time.

Blake had signed a two-way contract, allowing Nashville to move him back and forth between the minors and the NHL without notice. Fall turned to winter—Blake's fifth in Wisconsin, more than he had bargained for when the Predators took him with their first draft selection back in 2006. Katelyn wasn't far away, but she had chosen to enroll in law school rather than follow her boyfriend from city to city. She had always been driven, always independent, traits Blake had long admired.

Though they were separated by only about a hundred miles, the schedule of a professional player, even a minor league one, left little time for courting. In the same state where he had climbed to stardom, he was now back at the bottom.

The calendar rolled over, and on February 7, 2011, Blake was named the AHL Player of the Week for the second consecutive week—the first player to receive back-to-back honors in nearly two decades—after racking up thirteen points and a plus-eight rating in four games, including three assists and the game-winning goal the night after his twenty-third birthday. "It's not always the skill, it's the will," said Poile. "What Blake had going for him was a lot of determination and a strong hockey sense." The rumblings out of the Preds' fan base, nearly as exasperated with the delay as Blake himself, were growing louder by the day.

Coaches, general managers, fans, bloggers, sports bettors, and fantasy team owners obsess over injury reports, squinting at meager descriptions alongside player names. With the electronic flicker of an injury update, a hundred amateur physicians rattle off their dubious diagnoses. Yet no one obsesses like the minor leaguer waiting for a call-up. All he needs is an opportunity. Just one. For some, it never comes.

Blake's finally did on February 25, 2011, a seeming eternity after he squeezed into that Brentwood elementary school desk to mug for the cameras. One minute he was jostling through another minor league drill in Milwaukee, and the next he was fumbling his way into a dark Dallas hotel room, guided only by the titanic snores of his temporary roommate, Belarusian winger Sergei Kostitsyn. Long after Blake crawled beneath the sheets, he lay staring up at the dark ceiling, the latest in a long series of anonymous hotel rooms. Nothing was different, yet everything had changed.

∼

Seven minutes into the game against the Dallas Stars, Blake was sent over the boards with a sharp command from his new coach, NHL legend Barry Trotz. "Geoffrion, you're up."

He skated over to the face-off circle, settling low across from Steve Ott, the polyglot trash talker and sometimes-enforcer for the Stars. Blake's heart was in his throat when his ears perked up as a familiar voice cut through the din.

"Let me take this one."

Blake looked up and saw the grinning face of another former Badger captain, Adam Burish, now playing for Dallas. "Congrats, man. This is a great league, you're going to enjoy it."

The Badger camaraderie was contagious. "Hey Bur, let me win this draw."

"Oh yeah, man, no problem."

Blake adjusted his grip, eyes lowering and stick descending downward as the puck dropped from the referee's fingertips. He raked backward . . . through nothing. Looking up, he saw Burish skating back into the play and laughing over his shoulder. "Not a chance!"

Blake had long imagined his first NHL goal. So had many others. Dan Davidge, Blake's coach at Culver. Laura Trosper, who had taught toddler Blake to ice skate. Mike Eaves. Artie, the rink manager at the Kohl Center. All the kids who had lined up for autographs at Badger games. Ron DeGregorio at USA Hockey. Danny and Kelly. Blake's brothers, who had played goalie while he practiced in the backyard. The moment finally came in Edmonton, three days after his NHL debut.

The line changed on the fly, and another former Badger, Ryan Suter, carried the puck up the ice all the way into the offensive zone. Matt Halischuk, a step ahead of Blake, scooted to the right side, and Blake went to net, eyes darting from Suter behind the cage to Halischuk waiting on the wing. The blind pass from Suter dinged off Blake's skate, and he used his toe to nudge the puck out to his stick blade tip and roofed it clean into the net. A pause, hands half raised, and then the horn sounded and the lamp lit and the familiar crush of teammates closed around him. "Fuckin' A, right!" Blake yelled. "I can't believe that just happened!"

But Nashville trailed Detroit by six games in the Central Division, the Predators' veteran forwards weren't producing, and forty-seven minutes and fifteen seconds remained in the game. No time to sit back and reflect. Less than a minute later, Edmonton's Jim Vandermeer matched Blake's goal, and the two tallies stood lonely, side by side, through the rest of regulation and into overtime. Edmonton won the shootout, and an hour later the Predators were westbound for a matchup with Vancouver. *Welcome to the show, kid. Don't forget to save that puck.*

Three weeks later, on a chilly Sunday afternoon in March, Kevin Hagan, the president of Greater Nashville Area Scholastic Hockey, was driving home from his job as an insurance broker on the east side of Nashville. His radio was tuned to 102.5, WPRT-FM, and he listened as the jocular, smooth, and familiar voice of the Preds' play-by-play announcer, Pete Weber, began to climb with the excitement of an approaching scoring opportunity. As Weber exclaimed, "Geoffrion, with his second of the game!" Hagan leaned on the gas pedal, accelerating the car to keep time with his heartbeat. *Another goal! What happened with the first? Could this damn traffic move any slower?*

Hagan raced home and flipped on the TV, gathering his family to watch Tennessee hockey history unfold in real time. They would not be disappointed. Blake had staked Nashville to a 1–0 lead with a first-period goal, but the Predators had given up three unanswered in the second. With less than three minutes to go in the game, Blake barreled toward the net and started hacking away, sending a crossing pass that deflected off defender Paul Gaustad's skate past Buffalo goalie Ryan Miller. The Hagans watched, captivated, as the final minutes wound down, all eyes on young Blake, the manifestation of their southern hockey pride. He bullied his way back into the offensive zone and with 1:23 left on the clock tipped in a Cody Franson shot from the point to tie the game and seal his first professional hat trick. No matter that all three goals had been ugly, none of them coming on a shot. Middle Tennessee hockey fans declared it the *Preds-iest hat trick of all time.* As Blake leapt into the air and crashed ecstatically into the plexiglass, he heard a familiar voice, a little thickened with Labatt, boom, "That's my son!" Danny and his beer league hockey buddies danced and roared, stomping and shouting for the whole arena to hear.

"Blake was the torchbearer, he was the trendsetter, he was the groundbreaker," reflected Hagan. "Such a seminal event—to think a kid from Nashville could even play in the NHL."

Not just play but also score. And win. Martin Erat's overtime goal gave the Predators their third win in a row, and they added six of the next eight as well. Blake's third goal had been his seventh point in ten games. The Predators had clinched a playoff berth and were headed to Anaheim in pursuit of the first playoff series win in franchise history.

It had been more than a decade since Blake had lived at home. He was now a professional hockey player, but his folks had kept his room unchanged, the Team USA gold medal still hanging from the wall, and he moved back in. His return was reminiscent of a carefree college student's winter break. Mom cooked his meals and folded his laundry and tried her best not to wash his game jerseys with the whites.

And then, one morning at practice, he felt a hand on his shoulder and saw Trotz's eyes, glowering as he delivered the news: "We appreciate what you're doing. You've been playing really great." But we're going with the veterans for the playoff push." He would play bottom-six minutes only, scraping together a shift or two per game if he was lucky.

Blake was stunned. *Let the best players play!* he thought. The bitter taste remained in his mouth as he watched the Predators record their first-ever playoff series victory, defeating Anaheim in the Western Conference quarterfinals. The crowd went berserk, and Blake fist-bumped and smiled for the cameras, though he couldn't help but feel like a tourist just along for the ride.

The feeling lingered through the semifinals against Vancouver. He won a few face-offs, laid down a few hits, let loose a few shots on goal. Most important, he avoided silly rookie mistakes. The series was tight—

one-goal wins and overtime thrillers, back-to-back-to-back—but the big
moments belonged to the veterans, just as Trotz had intended.

Blake watched Game 6 with barely a hint of sweat under his jersey
as the Canucks ended the series with a Daniel Sedin scoring flourish.
"I felt like a plug, like a healthy scratch," Blake recalled. Danny had
been forced, reluctantly, back into the role of an observer. His first
NHL season was over. He wouldn't forget how it had ended.

Professional hockey felt different. For all the criticism of the NCAA
and its slide away from amateurism, college players still played for a
love of the game. The team felt like a team, and no one was out trying
to prove their worth for the next contract. Blake spent a lot of time
talking with Katelyn about it. "This is a very different type of team,"
he told her. "Here, it's every man for himself." He might have chosen
Wisconsin as his best shot to make the NHL, but somewhere along the
way, he had fallen for the amateur game. He missed it.

Still, Blake had proven that he could adapt, even if it took some time.
A slow start, then ascendancy, followed by adversity, followed by virtu-
osity. Rinse, cycle, repeat—at Culver, at USA Hockey, and in Madison.
Unmet expectations fermented within, bubbling up to put pressure
where needed. It was back to the gym, the practice rink, the drawing
board. Blake knew the recipe by heart.

Laughing, joking, breathing easily, Blake was cruising his way through
the second game of the 2011 preseason, a doubleheader against the Florida Panthers, the rigorous discipline of a buckle-down offseason already
paying dividends. "Blake realized that on off days, he had to work as
hard or harder than everybody else," recalled Poile. "It's not like he can
take his foot off the gas pedal and cruise."

Blake had already collected a goal and an assist in that matchup—the
rest of the season, a regular roster spot, and a steady uptick in ice time
beckoned. Cruising to the bench, he stepped over the half wall and
plopped down, the little corner scrum he'd just pushed his way out of

already forgotten. It was just another shift, like thousands before it. He felt good. Blake shook off his glove to cool down before his next shift, and blood gushed from a gaping wound on his wrist onto the sleeve of his white jersey. There was no pain, just surprise and bewilderment. He hadn't felt a thing.

The verdict was swift and unequivocal: a partially severed tendon, immediate suspension of all physical activity. Any increase in blood pressure and the thing could split in two. *Shit.*

Blake spent the next two weeks observing games and practices and weight room sessions in his street clothes, gingerly holding his injured wrist at an awkward angle. Sitting, waiting, watching as his muscles atrophied, all the hard-won conditioning slipping away. Blake had suffered his share of injuries, but he'd never really paused to consider that everything could go away in an instant. A lifetime of practices and runs and lifts and games and camps and tournaments had finally brought him a professional career. And it was all so precarious.

When his wrist healed and he returned to action, the carefree confidence so necessary to his game was gone. He didn't play poorly, but he didn't dazzle, and when the Opening Night roster was announced, his name was missing. Blake spent the fall and winter of 2011 bouncing back and forth between Milwaukee and Nashville, alternating between butting heads with the Admirals' new coach (a "fucking buffoon") and scraping together a few fourth-line minutes with the Predators and managing no more than a handful of assists. It wasn't the glitzy and glamorous professional life he had envisioned. But then, few first jobs are. When his phone rang in February, he answered testily.

It was Poile. "How are you doing, Blake?"

"I'm in the minors, David, how the fuck do you think I'm doing?"

"You've been traded."

"To where?"

Blake called his father. When Danny Geoffrion answered his phone, he couldn't believe what he heard. He stood in the bright Atlanta sunshine, his mother, Marlene, on his arm, the movie they had just seen erased from memory. For once, he kept his comments to himself, his head slumped a little toward his chest. "Why'd it have to be Montreal?" he thought.

Danny understood the passions and pressures of Montreal hockey better than most. He was born in January 1958, as the Canadiens were making a run to their eighth consecutive Stanley Cup finals appearance. Boom Boom scored the goal that clinched the championship. Danny had been raised on stories of Howie Morenz.

Danny Geoffrion had been a prodigy in the storied Quebec Major Junior Hockey League before being selected in the first round of the NHL draft by Montreal in 1978, but he instead chose to play for the World Hockey League's (WHL) Quebec Nordiques and escape the shadows cast by his father and grandfather. The WHL folded a year later, and he joined the Canadiens, who still held his professional rights. A week before the season started, Montreal brought in his father as head coach, but Boom Boom's tenure was short and unsuccessful. Though Danny remained on the team that his father had helped make famous, he never scored a goal in a Canadiens sweater.

The legendary Guy Lafleur once said, "When you win in Montreal, it's the best place in the world to play hockey." Longtime hockey executive and commentator Brian Burke put it differently: "The hardest part about playing in Montreal is that you suck in two languages."

When the Bell Centre sells out all 21,302 of its seats, as it did for 583 consecutive games beginning in 2004, it is said that 21,303 coaches are in attendance. The passion of the Canadiens' fan base is not merely a product of their history, though Montreal's captains have hoisted Lord Stanley's cup an unrivaled twenty-four times. Nor does it rely solely on the legion of titanic figures, predating the creation of the NHL, who have donned *la Sainte-Flanelle* with its *C* and *H*. Fan ardor results from these things and more—ethnic nationalism, Francophone pride and resentment—and creates potent pressures on the players who take to the ice to represent the *équipe national*, the national team, of a nation within a nation. Only on hockey nights are the Quebecoise equals. In victory, they are kings.

Boom Boom Geoffrion knew exactly what it meant to pull that sweater over his head. Five decades before his grandson donned the colors, Boom Boom was shouldering the reputation for winning passed down from Howie Morenz, Georges Vézina, and Maurice "Rocket" Richard. Geoffrion wasn't just shaking Richard's hand at rookie orientation but playing on a line with the Rocket, the living, breathing embodiment of Quebecois pride, hero of the late third period, the overtime, who always delivered the game winner when it was most needed.

With Richard, the homegrown product of working-class Montreal, one of their own, the Canadiens became unstoppable. The captain's eyes blazed with *le feu sacre*, the sacred fire. He could score goals, yes—the first to five hundred in the league's history. He could skate, erupting off the rush, searing through his opponents' blue line, leaving the opposing goalie naked and exposed and deflated even before the puck left his stick. He could—and did—fight. As the attacks grew nastier, so too did his retaliations, blood splattering freely from his knuckles and theirs. And French Canada adored him for it. NHL president Clarence Campbell began to levy heavier and heavier fines on Richard as the incidents mounted. Canadiens fans gleefully paid up, taking up collections and mailing them directly to the league's offices.

On March 13, 1955, Richard landed the biggest blow of his career, squarely on the face of Cliff Thompson, a linesman working the Bruins–Canadiens matchup. Thompson fell to the ice unconscious, and the rink exploded into violence.

After the game ended, the great captain sat in the dressing room drenched in blood and sweat, the visible carnage a shock to his hovering teammates. Then *bang! Bang! Bang!* the sound of the Boston police hammering at the door echoed around him. They had come to arrest

Richard on assault charges, but his teammates, among them Boom Boom Geoffrion, kept the entryway blocked. That evening, Richard was whisked north across the border to safety.

Having escaped the clutches of Boston's police and the balled fists of the Bruins fan base, Richard had one more gauntlet to run. What happened next became part of Canadiens lore, a story to be passed on to new generations of fans and new crops of players for decades to come. On March 16, Campbell, who represented everything Anglo, superior, and condescending to French Canada, summoned Richard and team representatives to a hearing. The verdict wasn't long in coming: Richard was suspended, not only for the remaining three regular-season games but also for the playoffs. The Rocket was leading the league in points, poised to win his first scoring title. The man hot on his heels in the points standings? Geoffrion.

The next day, the Habs were scheduled to host the Red Wings. Crowds gathered hours before the puck was set to drop, with furious fans carrying signs that protested the injustice visited on their hero.

Vive Richard, Vive le Rocket. Tu as péché, Campbell.

Campbell, notorious for his punctuality, strolled down the steps to his seat six minutes into the first period, his secretary on his arm. The atmosphere inside the arena was heavy, nearly flammable. Spectators hurled insults at the league president, soon adding to their arsenal tomatoes, rotten eggs, pennies, peanuts, and programs. Campbell sat resolutely in his somber suit and tie, calmly carrying on amid the barrage, until someone in the stands set off a tear gas canister, sending him and the rest of the attendees to the exits.

Clarence was burned in effigy on the sidewalk outside. Thousands dressed in blue, white, and red had turned their signs into kindling, and paper and wood crackled in showers of sparks. Someone kicked in a storefront window, and within minutes the sound of tinkling glass meeting pavement reverberated up and down rue Sainte-Catherine. The cars were next—several exploded in fireballs, and the mob rocked police vehicles holding handcuffed rioters, officers and protesters alike gripping desperately to the door handles, knuckles whitening and hearts leaping as the explosions of nearby automobiles echoed. Bottles smashed through the windows of streetcars halted amid the fray. A bullet shattered the front windows of the Forum. Madness had overtaken Montreal.

In all, more than one hundred people were arrested, many with pockets stuffed full of looted jewelry. The Richard Riot turned their soft-spoken hockey captain into a folk hero.

That weekend, the Quebec nationalist paper *Le Devoir* ran an editorial under the headline "On a Tué Mon Frère Richard" (They have killed my brother Richard).

> French-Canadian nationalism appears to have taken refuge in hockey. The crowds that vented their anger last Thursday night were not motivated solely by the passions of sport or an injustice committed against an idol. It was a frustrated people who protested against their fate.

The tale of the Richard Riot and the Quiet Revolution that it helped to ignite was the type of history that Danny Geoffrion had left behind when he moved to the United States. He taught his sons to shoot and skate, to love their family and be proud of their name. But he didn't teach them to speak French or to think about hockey as an expression of provincial or ethnic pride. It was a game, and that was enough.

Bernie Geoffrion was a direct descendant of Pierre Joffrion and Marie Priault, two French settlers who had arrived in the colony of Montreal in the 1660s. Boom Boom was *pure laine*, pure wool, French Canadian through and through, and at the age of twenty-four, he had already played a significant role in cementing Montreal's place in the league as a perennial contender and in the hearts of Quebecois as a source of regional and ethnic honor. Playing on a line with Richard and Jean Béliveau, Boom Boom had helped the Habs win a Stanley Cup in 1953.

Two nights after the Richard Riot, Geoffrion recorded a goal and two assists, his seventy-fourth, seventy-fifth, and seventy-sixth points of the season. Richard's season had ended at seventy-five. Geoffrion thus became just the second Canadien to win the scoring title.

The Montreal fans loved Boom Boom. They loved his charisma, so very French, just as they loved his magnificent slap shot. But, in the words of longtime referee and official Red Storey, hockey in Quebec "was bigger than the Church, and Rocket Richard was bigger than the Pope." Boom Boom's scoring title was an affront to the symbol of *Richard* much more than to the man *Maurice* at a time of umbrage and shame for all of French Canada. As Geoffrion skated back to the bench, the scoreboard blinking the truth of his crowning achievement, the same fans who so often cheered his successes now jeered. He was sickened by the scorn. "I couldn't deliberately not score," he complained after the game. "That isn't the point of hockey, Montreal." The fans didn't care. In Montreal, they punished just as intensely as they rewarded. *Vive le Rocket.*

Danny Geoffrion was born three years after the Richard Riot, and he grew up knowing that fans had booed his dad for winning the scoring title. The same pressure that had sickened Boom Boom both as a player and as a coach helped drive Danny out of professional hockey entirely.

The minute he heard where Blake had been traded, the history and the memories came rushing back. Danny wanted to be happy for his son. He could sense the excitement in Blake's voice, not just at the much-needed change of scenery but at the opportunity to continue a family legacy eighty-nine years in the making. So Danny said nothing, just wished his son the best, as he always had, a proud father knowing that even if he wanted to, he couldn't protect his child from the world.

Blake's reaction to the news was threefold: betrayal, relief, excitement. Betrayed by the team that had drafted and developed him only to ship him off like a bag of meat at the trade deadline. Relieved to be getting out of the bad situation in which he was stuck, with a minor-league coach he didn't respect. Excited that he would continue his career in a place where his family had toiled for generations. His father's trepidation never crossed his mind.

Habs fire coach Jacques Martin, *CBC Sports*, Dec. 17, 2011
  Montreal Canadiens didn't play with enough desperation, *Sportsnet*,
Feb. 1, 2012
  Canadiens great Beliveau in hospital after stroke, *WLTX*,
Feb. 28, 2012
  Canadiens apologize for hiring a coach who doesn't speak French,
Boston Globe, Jan. 3, 2012

Yes, Pierre Gauthier, Montreal's general manager, had committed the
unpardonable sin of employing a head coach who was a monoglot, and
an Anglophone at that. "It felt like he was set up to fail," recalled Max
Pacioretty, the team's star and later captain.

Pacioretty's frustration had been building for some time. The team was
plodding along to a last-place finish in the Eastern Conference and its
first season without a playoff appearance in five years. The Canadiens
were riddled with problems, not the least of which was the Montreal
tradition of carrying Francophone players on the fourth line even if
they weren't up to the standards of the modern NHL.

Randy Cunneyworth, the newly hired Frenchless head coach scrambling to learn a foreign language while steering the ship of the most
storied, most scrutinized franchise in hockey history, didn't last long. The
team just could not win. Each successive loss only intensified the eager-
ness to see Blake Geoffrion in a Habs sweater. The Montreal hockey
press salivated at the return of the storied name to their market. Sportsnet christened him Baby Boom. NHL.com declared "a legacy fulfilled"
before he'd played a single shift wearing the Montreal colors.

For the fans, there was a poetry to his homecoming. Many had watched
him play in the World Juniors, battling against Jonathan Toews and
Carey Price in that haunting 2007 semifinal. "Canadians are like the
Irish in a sense," said hockey historian Andrew Holman. "If you have
any kind of bloodline or inheritance, despite what you call yourself,
deep down you're still Canadian." Or in this case Canadien.

He did not disappoint. In a week and a half with Montreal's minor
league affiliate in late February, Blake collected two goals and five assists

in five games. The suits in the front office decided they had waited long
enough. Blake would officially join the team on the road the following
week. What number would he like to wear?

The last time he had stepped on the ice at the Bell Centre, on March
11, 2006, he had watched two numbers and two beloved names rise above
the weeping crowd. He would wear 57—5 for Boom Boom, his Pappy,
and 7 for his great-grandfather Howie Morenz. Although Blake didn't
know it, March 11 was the anniversary of other somber endings in the
shared history of the Montreal Canadiens franchise and the Geoffrion/
Morenz family: ten years before his grandfather's death, the Canadiens
had played their final game at the Montreal Forum on March 11, 1996.
And on March 11, 1937, Howie Morenz had been laid out in the Forum
in the only funeral ever conducted on the eminent ice sheet.

In his sixth game as a Canadien, with time winding down in the second period of a road matchup against the Vancouver Canucks, Blake

Blake as a member of the Montreal Canadiens follows through
on a shot against the Tampa Bay Lightning.
Photograph by Mike Carlson, Reuters, 2012.

caught a slick pass on his stick blade as it crossed the crease, deflecting the puck into the goal. No flash, no dazzle, just the right place at the right time, at home in front of the cage once again. As he skated away, the numbers on the back of his jersey pressed hot against his skin. Back in Quebec, fans cheered in English and French. They would have to wait just a little longer to see another Geoffrion goal in person.

Gauthier was seeing exactly what he had hoped for when he brought a Geoffrion back to Montreal and sent a two-year contract extension to Blake's agent. But Gauthier was fired on March 29, replaced as general manager by Marc Bergevin, who took one look around and announced loudly (in French) that he wasn't honoring old contracts. "You want to make my team, you'll go down to the minors," he told Blake. And then, over the summer of 2012, collective-bargaining negotiations collapsed.

Blake had expected to spend at most a week or two in the minor leagues, just as he had when he joined Montreal at the trade deadline. Instead, like the rest of the hockey world, he was left waiting, indefinitely on pause until the NHL and the players' union could reach a deal.

Stu Cowan, the tireless sports editor for the *Montreal Gazette*, was enjoying a rare off night at the Bell Centre. It was November, the NHL lockout was two months old, and many veterans had signed temporary contracts in Europe. Younger players stuck on two-way contracts were laboring in the minor leagues. With the Bell Centre empty, the Canadiens starved for revenue, and their fans pining for hockey, what better use for the old barn could there be than letting the up-and-comers play a game on the big stage on Friday night? Cowan was sitting about twenty rows up from the ice with his son, savoring the return of professional hockey to Montreal, even if it was only a minor league matchup. Cowan welcomed the swish of skates, and when No. 57 took the ice, he cheerfully launched into an explanation of Geoffrion family history.

Danny and Kelly Geoffrion were sitting a few sections away. En route from Nashville to Massachusetts, where one of Blake's brothers, Sebastian, was playing against Northeastern University, the proud hockey parents decided to stop and watch Blake take the ice in Danny's home-town against the Syracuse Crunch. It was reminiscent of the old days, when they had shuttled their boys from one rink to the next across the South, sometimes playing four or five games a weekend. Pee Wees, bantams, prep school, college, pros. For the parents, the distinctions matter less.

They watched Blake stand up for his next shift, hop back onto the ice, then take that pass along the boards, a smile crossing Danny's face as Blake accelerated, teasing the puck forward at the end of his stick. But they saw what Blake didn't: Jean-Philippe Côté barreling across the ice, shoulder leveled and legs coiled for a check aimed at Blake's right shoulder. They watched the hit, watched as it sent Blake rag-dolling through the air, then crashing down flat on his back, his head snapping backward to collide with Côté's upturned skate blade, which slipped past his ear and his helmet strap and dug deep into his skull.

Blake's teammates punched and shoved Côté, but Habs trainer Gra-ham Rynbend and rink-side trauma surgeon Daniel Deckelbaum ignored the fisticuffs as they helped Blake off the ice. Once in the trainer's room, Deckelbaum removed the helmet and clamped a thick gauze pad against the side of Blake's head, where blood gushed through his hair. The sur-geon began his routine examination, then looked up and calmly said, "We need to get this guy to a hospital. I suspect a skull fracture." His gloved fingers had slid easily through the gaping hole, through the muscle and into the skull. Blake's brain was exposed.

Danny's first thought had been, *Oh, great, another concussion.* He hadn't seen the skate go through Blake's skull. He had seen the blood on the ice, but he had also watched Blake stand up, his arm dangling as if his shoulder had been separated. Danny and Kelly sat, concerned but not fearful, as play resumed, though she whispered a prayer under her breath, just in case. They did not expect the team to call with updates.

But then Danny's phone rang.

"Is this Daniel Geoffrion?" asked an unfamiliar voice. "What section are you in? We've got people coming to get you right now. We're taking Blake to the hospital."

Strapped to a spine board, Blake was hustled into an ambulance. Kelly climbed into the back with him, while Danny sat next to the driver up front, fingernails digging into the dashboard as the vehicle lurched forward. The side trip to Quebec had morphed into a nightmare.

Kelly held her son's hand as the sirens wailed through the streets of Montreal. Seeing him in the back of the ambulance, his head encased in yellow foam, her heart had jumped with fear. Restraints were immobilizing Blake, but he could talk and he could see the panic dancing across her face. It wasn't a concussion; she had seen too many of those to mistake the signs. He tried to reassure her that he was fine, making a point of talking, joking, and laughing as the ambulance raced through one stoplight after another. His mother began to breathe normally again.

"Do you want me to call Katelyn?" she asked. Blake and Katelyn were now engaged.

"Oh god, no," Blake replied. "She'll think it's my head, she'll just worry." Kelly smiled weakly back at him. Blake could always make her smile.

When they arrived at the hospital, she and Danny sat in the waiting room as the doctors ran routine tests on her boy. The medical staff had repeatedly reassured the anxious parents that Blake was there as a precaution, nothing more. She idly flipped through a magazine until a breathless nurse said, "Madame, Madame, we need your signature! He iz going into surgery!"

"Why?" asked Kelly.

"He iz seizing right now!"

Fear again enveloped Kelly.

When Kelly and Danny peered through the glass of the ICU window, their son's reassuring smile was gone, replaced by a breathing tube as he lay, sedated and prepped for surgery, under the fluorescent hospital lights. Three doctors swept by in their white coats, pausing for a moment to explain that a lot depended on how much his brain had swelled. They didn't know whether he would talk again or walk again or have any memory at all. "Will he live?" his parents asked. They didn't know that, either.

Fragments of skull were laying on his brain lining, and they needed to get him on the operating table. Immediately.

Danny and Kelly sat side-by-side in the waiting room, taking turns sobbing until the tears no longer came and then shaking silently. Danny insisted that she call the other boys.

"And tell them what?" she replied. "We don't even know if he'll be alive in the morning."

∾

Dr. Mohammad Maleki, the director of the neurotrauma service at Montreal General, performed the surgery, acting quickly to relieve swelling and pressure from the accumulation of blood and other fluids against Blake's brain. Using a scalpel and then a bone saw, Maleki made a large, C-shaped incision in the left side of Blake's skull, extracted the one-inch portion of skull that had been crushed by the steel of the whirling skate, scraped the lining of the brain to remove any bone fragments, and then covered the hole with a metal mesh plate, which was screwed into place. The surgery stretched on for nearly four hours.

From the waiting room, Kelly called Katelyn, who was enjoying a night off from her law school studies, sharing a bottle of wine with childhood friends and having forgotten exactly where Blake was playing that night.

But when Katelyn answered the phone, Kelly was immediately called away. "Stay by your phone, I'll be right back," she told her son's fiancée. Sensing the panic in Kelly's voice, Katelyn put her phone on speaker and desperately began scrolling through Twitter, searching for Blake's name. There it was: *Blake Geoffrion injured badly and rushed to a Montreal hospital after taking a check . . .* White noise began to hiss in her head.

A male voice came through the phone, unnaturally loud: "You need to prepare yourselves. After the seizure, we brought him right into surgery. It's the brain; we don't know how it's going yet."

The rest was lost as static roared in Katelyn's ears. The room spun. She ran to the bathroom, sank to her knees, and dry heaved into the toilet.

Her parents picked her up that night and put her on a plane to Montreal the next morning, despite her near-catatonic state. Danny called her when she landed. He explained that Blake had woken up after surgery and been frantic, trying to pull the ventilator tube out of his throat. He had first been restrained by nurses and orderlies and then sedated.

But when he awoke again, Blake had brain function. Lying in bed, with his parents, team owner Geoff Molson, and Marc Bergevin all standing around him, he had written two words on a notepad: "Where's Katelyn?"

She arrived at the hospital to find her fiancé asleep, wired to a dozen frightening machines, the ventilator tube back in his throat. As she looked down at him, his eyes flickered open. He saw her and burst into tears. Then his eyes closed as he slipped back into unconsciousness. On the stand next to his hospital bed lay the notepad, on which he had scribbled a new question.

"When can I play again?"

~

Over the weeks that followed, more people came to wish him well, to root for him in his recovery as they had in his time on the ice. So many, in fact, that when he was transferred to another hospital under an alias, George Benson.

"Hockey in Montreal is more than a religion," reflected Deckelbaum. "Blake's status, recovery was all over the media, and when it comes to injury, people are quite understanding of players and families. They want so badly to show their support and solidarity." The fans had clasped his hands on the day Pappy died, had thrust forward Boom Boom memorabilia for Blake's signature when he was traded to their beloved franchise, had clapped him on the back and assured him that there was no place in the world to play hockey like Montreal. Now they tented their fingers in prayer for a return to health.

The days slipped by, and with each new doctor, Blake asked the question that dominated his waking thoughts: "Am I done?" He finally demanded that Katelyn show him the gash across his head. The photo she showed him revealed an enormous horseshoe-shaped scar, like the bloody crack lines across the shell of a broken egg.

After that, he stopped asking.

When Blake was discharged from the hospital, the team put him, Katelyn, and Kelly up in the Queen Elizabeth, a grand hotel that had opened its doors in April 1958, five days before Boom Boom Geoffrion scored the winning goal in the Stanley Cup finals. The well-wishers and reporters remained so numerous that the team stationed an armed guard at the door. The grandeur of the hotel's classic lobby, its white marble floors and sweeping staircases, was lost on them. So were the sights along René Lévesque Boulevard, along which the three trudged every day, Katelyn and Kelly supporting Blake between them. Weeks passed before he was strong enough to traverse the entire block, all three hundred feet of it. Sapped of energy, he would return to bed, sleep for twelve, thirteen hours, then doze for the rest of the day. Friends and teammates stopped by—Max Pacioretty, the Canadiens' captain who had suffered a traumatic injury the year before, brought his wife, Katia, and a box of chocolates, which Blake shoveled into his mouth as fast as he could. Brian Burke, general manager of the Toronto Maple Leafs, took him to breakfast in the hotel restaurant. Burke's youngest son had been killed in a car accident two years earlier. Everyone had encouragement. No one had answers.

The exhaustion and the forced bed rest gave Blake time to think. He had spent his lifetime pursuing a dream, and what had it really been like once he'd achieved it? He realized that he had been too in awe of the NHL, had given too much respect to the other pros; that attitude had kept him from just playing his game the way he should have. He recognized that he'd been kept out of games not because he didn't deserve a spot in the lineup but so that the team could reduce his service time and keep control over his contract, the ugly side of the hockey business that Danny had muttered about from time to time. And he knew that hockey was only getting faster, that the pace of the game and the speed of the players was headed in only one direction. What he didn't know—what no one knew—was whether these revelations were about Blake's present and future or his past. Would he take to the ice again, wiser than before, better equipped to survive as a professional and win as a player? Or had the lessons come too late to be useful, the pocket lint of a career cut short?

~

More than a month passed before Blake was allowed to fly. On board the plane back to the United States, Katelyn couldn't stop staring at him, worried that the change in air the pressure would cause his head to explode. It didn't.

Back in Chicago, where the two had bought a home the previous year, some semblance of normal returned. He spent Christmas with his family in Brentwood, the first time in years that he had been able to enjoy the holiday at his parents' home. On December 31, the William-son County, Tennessee, newspaper ran an article headlined with a quote from Kelly: "God is good to the Geoffrions." Marc Bergevin returned to the Canadiens' front office; Jean-Philippe Côté laced up his skates and headed back onto the ice. Even Katelyn, who had refused to leave his side for weeks on end at the hospital, resumed studying in the law school library.

But for Blake, there was no return. The only life he had ever known, had ever envisioned, was on the ice. That competitiveness had gotten him everywhere he had ever wanted to go. During a game that he shouldn't have suited up for, in a season that never happened, it was also what had gotten him hurt.

The agony of his shattered life plan was compounded by the blinding pain that wracked his skull, pain that had only gotten worse since his return to the States. When Katelyn left the house each morning, Blake turned off all the lights, closed every blind and shade, and sat in the shower, letting the hot water run straight onto his head. It was the only thing that eased the migraines. When the water turned cold, he rose to his feet, stepped gingerly out of the shower, toweled off, and sat in the dark, waiting for the water to heat up again. And swallowing the many painkillers he had been prescribed.

The nights were no better. His sleep was fitful and broken. His brain, the engine of his good nature, his endless competitiveness, his intensity and drive in everything he did, was betraying him.

He occasionally called friends, old teammates, just to have something to do. Yet there was a déjà vu element to the conversations, at least to those on the receiving end, who were deeply unsettled by Blake's short-term memory loss.

"I'd talk to him one day," recalled Ryan McDonagh, now playing for the Rangers, "and then he'd call back the next day and we would have the exact same conversation. He didn't remember calling me in the first place."

Blake's nonhockey friends had gradually been falling away since elementary school. He had given up all the normal adolescent experiences. All his buddies were still playing.

Katelyn was working and studying from eight in the morning to eight at night. She tried to come up with tasks to keep Blake occupied and casual conversation topics to keep the mood light. With their wedding day approaching, she assigned him responsibility for the invitations and all that came with it—finding a calligrapher, picking up the completed envelopes, licking, sealing, stamping. It kept him busy for a few days, but once the invitations were mailed, quiet descended on their house again. He was mourning the loss of hockey.

Blake had always been a talker, determined to chase away silence. As the weeks turned to months and he lapsed further into quiet, one unspoken rumination boomed loudly in his brain. The thought ate at him, over and over. *You could end it.*

Three NHL players had died of nonnatural causes over the previous year in what came to be called hockey's annus horribilis, the horrible year. Derek Boogaard died on May 13, 2011, of an overdose of alcohol and oxycodone. His parents donated their son's brain to Boston University to be examined for signs of chronic traumatic encephalopathy (CTE). While they awaited the results, two more NHL veterans took their own lives—Rick Rypien on August 15 and Wade Belak on August 31. All three had been enforcers, veterans of dozens of minor hockey and professional fights as well as the thousands of body checks and blocked shots and concussions that come with any extended career in the game. Their deaths shed new light on the use and misuse of prescription painkillers in the NHL. "Percocets," said one player, "are golden in the hockey world."

The American public health epidemic caused by overprescription of opioids was still not fully understood. In 2011, 259 million prescriptions were written for opioids in the United States—one for every adult in the country. An estimated 2.1 million people became addicted.[1] The hard-hitting world of hockey is no different. "At the end of the day, the NHL is fighting the pharmaceutical industry," former Philadelphia Flyer Riley Cote told a magazine at the time. "You hear about it all the time—somebody injures a hand and winds up with a prescription for 30 Percocet and two refills. Worse, these painkillers mask your emotional pain."

Months after his injury, Blake finally confided in Katelyn about his depression. The doctors had warned her to expect it, and she had been watching him closely. Nevertheless, his admission terrified her. She had spent hours reading depositions from class action lawsuits involving athlete brain damage. She knew the statistics about player suicides. She had talked with the doctors, listened to their prognostications, researched the dense medical terminology, and kept vigilant watch over his moods. And despite all her efforts, the man with whom she wanted to spend the rest of her life was contemplating ending his own.

She recognized that more help was needed than she could offer—expert help. Katelyn managed to book an appointment with Dr. Julian Bailes, a neurosurgeon noted for his work with NFL players and pioneer in CTE research. As a summer associate at a law firm, she had researched class action lawsuits by former players suing the NFL and NHL and had come across Bailes's testimony in some of those cases.

Bailes recommended that Blake discontinue all painkillers—especially since they weren't killing the pain—and substituted a program of natural treatments. The doctor also praised the honesty between the couple. And Bailes reminded them that although little could be done to repair a brain, Blake had been fortunate to escape with minimal lasting damage. Time and physical therapy would help with the pain. Finally, the doctor had a somewhat unusual prescription: get a dog, a reason to get out of the house and walk, breaking up life between doctors' visits and tests and thoughts of the only game he had ever known, of a legacy lost.

Blake had always been a coachable player, and he threw himself into Dr. Bailes's regimen as just as intensely as he had embraced any on-ice practice schedule. He quit the painkillers cold turkey, a feat he was able to manage after years of forcing his unwilling body to comply with his stubborn brain. Many months, even years, of therapy and physical rehabilitation awaited him, but with the dam of silence broken, Blake shed the enormous weight of the depression that he had been carrying for months.

Improvement was slow, but it gradually came. The headaches became less constant and less severe. Dr. Bailes was right about that, and he was right about the rest, too. Blake and Katelyn found a French bulldog, George, his name taken from the alias Blake had used in Montreal, and the "little fucker saved my life."

At the beginning of March, a few weeks after meeting with Dr. Bailes, Blake and Katelyn flew to Mexico. It was the first vacation they had ever taken together, and for Blake, it was his first real time away from the game since he was a kid. He had left home at fourteen for military school and a shot at the NHL and never really paused to consider anything else. The two spent a week on the beach, swimming, relaxing, and talking about everything—everything except hockey. The interlude offered Blake a glimpse into what life outside the game could be. On the last day of their trip, he took Katelyn's hand and told her, "I think I'm done." Katelyn smiled, tears in her eyes. *A blessing in disguise*, she thought. That night, Montreal beat Tampa Bay, rallying to score three unanswered goals late in the third period. Neither Blake nor Katelyn watched.

The average NHL career lasts four and a half years. Some players have called the end of their playing days an abrupt reality check; others have described it as a traumatic moment. Struggles to come to terms with the lack of structure, the end to an all-consuming pursuit, leave former players bouncing from job to job, drinking too much, socializing too little. Most lack college degrees. The NHL and the players' union have recognized these challenges and have formalized counseling programs designed for ex-players. All players, the league and the union recognize, need help. Few of them have a Katelyn.

When they returned to the States, Blake was ready to speak his decision out loud. He called Marc Bergevin and broke the news. "I just lost it when I told him," he recalled.

As a player, Blake was done with hockey forever. His story had begun not when he had first laced up his skates or been drafted or scored his first goal as a Badger or a Predator or a Hab but ninety years earlier, when Howie Morenz had first pulled on a Montreal sweater. It had continued when Morenz was laid out on the ice of the Montreal Forum, when Boom Boom passed Richard to win the scoring title, and when Danny flamed out as a player but returned to Montreal to eulogize his father on March 11, the day the Canadiens retired his number.

Blake ended his call with Bergevin, tears pouring down his face. He felt regret, relief, release, and closure. He set down his phone, and the date blinked up at him.

It was March 11.

EPILOGUE

Following the international success of USA Hockey in the 2000s, the US National Team Development Program was recognized as an acclaimed model for elite player development. The program's success is as notable in hardware as it is in draft picks. Since 2010, USA Hockey has brought home four World Junior Championship gold medals and six U18 World Championship gold medals to Colorado Springs. In 2019, seventeen players from the NTDP U18 team were selected in the NHL draft, eight of them in the first round, a record number from any single team. Since the early 2010s, an average of fifty-five American players have been chosen in the NHL draft each year.

The University of Wisconsin–Madison men's hockey team has not returned to the NCAA national championship game since 2010. In 2021, the team qualified for the NCAA tournament after securing the regular season conference title but lost to Bemidji State in the first round. The Badgers' leading scorer was Cole Caufield, who received the Hobey Baker Award, only the second in program history. He did not accept the award in person, having already signed a professional contract with the Montreal Canadiens. He made his pro debut on April 9, the same day the award was announced.

Over the same time period, the Badger women's hockey team has won four national championships and appeared in two other national championship games. The squad is coached by Badger Bob's son, Mark

Johnson, who was considered but ultimately passed over for the men's team head coaching position in 2002. Over the next two decades, Johnson guided his team to seven national championships.

Hockey watchers widely acknowledge that the collective-bargaining agreement negotiated following the 2004–5 NHL lockout fundamentally changed the game. The implementation of the salary cap and the changes in the rules have increased the league's demand for younger, faster skaters. Skilled college players continue to depart college hockey before exhausting their eligibility, leaving college hockey to continue to grapple with the implications. Since 2010, six programs have won their first national championships—Massachusetts, Minnesota-Duluth, Providence, Quinnipiac, Union, and Yale—while only two have been won by traditional college hockey powerhouses. Five of those first-time-champion schools have fewer enrolled students than the Kohl Center has seats.

The short- and long-term effects of concussions and other traumatic brain injuries in organized hockey continue to be studied. One 2018 study found that women's hockey players reported concussions at a higher rate than professional football players, although underreporting of concussions remains an issue across the sporting world. John Branch's *Boy on Ice: The Life and Death of Derek Boogaard* and Ken Dryden's *Game Change: The Life and Death of Steve Montador, and the Future of Hockey* remain essential reading on the topics of injury, brain trauma, depression, and substance abuse in hockey.[1] The NHL has taken steps to reduce blind-side hits and implement new, more vigorous concussion protocols. In 2018, the league reached a settlement with more than one hundred ex-players pursuing a lawsuit alleging that the NHL did not do enough to prevent brain trauma or appropriately warn its players of risks.

Revelations regarding the insular nature of organized hockey and the toxicity it can allow or encourage have led to self-examination and fall-out among hockey players, coaches, administrators, and others close to the sport. In addition to Evan F. Moore and Jashvina Shah's *Game Misconduct: Hockey's Toxic Culture and How to Fix It*, Patrick O'Sullivan's essay "Black & Blue," published in the *Players Tribune*, offers a call to action for those struggling with the question of when and how to intervene in abusive situations.[2] The compassionate platform provided by TSN for Kyle Beach to tell his story of sexual assault at the hands of a Chicago Blackhawks trainer was an invaluable element of ongoing sport-wide revelations. Fredrik Backman's *Beartown* offers a fictional but deeply moving and insightful account of these issues within the game of hockey.[3]

Following his retirement in 2013, Blake Geoffrion worked as a scout and front office executive for several NHL organizations, including a stint as an assistant to Florida Panthers general manager Bill Zito, Blake's former agent. For several years, he hosted the Blake Geoffrion Hockey Classic in Madison, Wisconsin, a charity game and fundraiser for the UW Health Burn Center that featured former Badgers turned professional athletes and Olympians. He remains a regular speaker at USA Hockey camps and NTDP initiations. In September 2021, Blake was inducted into the University of Wisconsin Athletic Hall of Fame.

Blake and Katelyn married in August 2012, and their first child was born in 2016. According to Katelyn, she shares her father's energy and intensity. Her name is Blake.

NOTES

PROLOGUE

1. Bill Shaikin, "Donald Fehr Puts the Players First, This Time in Hockey," *Los Angeles Times*, December 17, 2012.

CHAPTER 1. WILLIAMSON COUNTY

1. Chris Palko, "America's Top 20 Conservative-Friendly Counties," *Daily Caller*, March 19, 2010, https://dailycaller.com/2010/03/19/americas-top-20-con servative-friendly-counties.

2. Mike Herron, quoted in David Hill, "The Union Forever," *Grantland*, March 1, 2013, grantland.com/features/hockey-tennessee-face-social-economic -change.

3. Jonathon Jackson, *The Making of Slap Shot: Behind the Scenes of the Greatest Hockey Movie Ever Made* (Hoboken, NJ: John Wiley, 2011), 17.

4. Chas Sisk, "How Nashville's Love of Hockey Began, Decades before the Predators," WPLN, June 2, 2017, https://wpln.org/post/how-nashvilles-love-of -hockey-began-decades-before-the-predators.

CHAPTER 3. FINDING WISCONSIN

1. Tim Rappleye, "3 Missing Anecdotes from Hobey Baker's Traditional Biography," *FloHockey*, FloSports, April 8, 2021, https://www.flohockey.tv/arti -cles/6959524-3-missing-anecdotes-from-hobey-bakers-traditional-biography.

2. Organized hockey has only just begun to grapple with elements of a subculture of toxicity long unacknowledged within the sport. For more on this subject, see Evan F. Moore and Jashvina Shaw, *Game Misconduct: Hockey's*

Toxic Culture and How to Fix It (Chicago: Triumph Books, 2021). Moore and Shaw examine a culture of insularity that they found to encourage playing and training through injury, to foster racism and homophobia, to enable drug and alcohol abuse, and to support cover-ups of misconduct, including sexual assault. *Legacy on Ice* is not intended as a comprehensive examination of these issues, and readers are encouraged to learn more through Moore and Shaw's work and elsewhere.

CHAPTER 5. THE PROS, AND THE END

1. For more information on the US opioid crisis and the role overprescription played in its origins, see Sam Quinones, *Dreamland: The True Tale of America's Opiate Epidemic* (New York: Bloomsbury, 2014).

EPILOGUE

1. John Branch, *Boy on Ice: The Life and Death of Derek Boogaard* (Toronto: HarperCollins, 2015); Ken Dryden, *Game Change: The Life and Death of Steve Montador, and the Future of Hockey* (Toronto: McClelland & Stewart, 2019).

2. Patrick O'Sullivan, "Black & Blue," *Players' Tribune*, December 10, 2015, https://www.theplayerstribune.com/articles/patrick-osullivan-nhl-abuse.

3. Fredrik Backman, *Beartown*, trans. Neil Smith (New York: Simon & Schuster, 2018).